✂ **W9-AGL-209**

The Banker and the Fisherman reminds us that real financial success is measured in more than just dollars and cents.

> - Ron Baron
>   Founder and CEO,
>   The Baron Funds

Gardening is an apt metaphor for what Ron Rogé does. The gardener prepares today for an uncertain future, but by planting in just the right space and feeding regularly, by quietly and consistently managing the risks of both drought and downpour, he brings forth abundance just when you need it most. Plan and be fruitful. Read and be inspired.

> - James J. Green
>   Editorial Director,
>   Investment Advisor and
>   Wealth Manager magazines

Ron Rogé offers readers an excellent reminder that there is much more to life than simply pursuing wealth.

> - Jeff Benjamin
>   Senior Editor,
>   Investment News

THE
BANKER
— and the —
Fisherman

THE

BANKER
— and the —
Fisherman

LESSONS IN LIFE, HAPPINESS, AND
WEALTH FOR THE 21ST CENTURY

Ronald W. Rogé

with Rosanne Rogé & Steven M. Rogé

Sherpa Publishing

Bohemia, New York

Certified Financial Planner (CFP®) is a registered trademark of the Certified Financial Planner® Board of Standards. All rights reserved. Chartered Mutual Fund Counselor (CMFC®) is a registered trademark of the College of Financial Planning. Certified Senior Advisor (CSA®) is a registered trademark of the Society of Certified Senior Advisors. Registered Financial Gerontologist (RFGSM) is a service mark of the American Institute of Financial Gerontology. Gratitude Focus™ is a copyright and trademark concept owned by The Strategic Coach® Inc. All rights reserved. Used with written permission. The D.O.S. Conversation and R-Factor Question are registered trademarks of The Strategic Coach® Inc. All rights reserved. Used with written permission. www.strategiccoach.com

ISBN 978-0-9820082-3-2

Publisher's Cataloging-in-Publication data

Rogé, Ronald W.
   The banker and the fisherman : lessons in life, happiness, and wealth for the 21st century / Ronald W. Rogé, Rosanne Rogé, and Steven M. Rogé.
   p. cm.
   ISBN 978-0-9820082-3-2
   Includes index.

      1. Finance, Personal. 2. Investments. 3. Estate planning -- United States. 4. United States -- Economic conditions. 5. Retirement -- United States -- Planning. 6. Older people -- Finance, personal. 7. Retirement -- Economic aspects -- United States. 8. Retirement income -- United States -- Planning. 9. Older people --Care -- United States -- Planning. I. The banker and the fisherman : lessons in life, happiness, and wealth for the twenty-first century. II. Title.

HG179 .R568 2008   332.024/01 21   dc22   2008906861

First Edition

Sherpa Publishing Inc.
630 Johnson Ave., Suite 103
Bohemia, NY 11716

Printed in Canada

To my high school chemistry teacher, Frank Siracusa, who took the time to care.

To Dan Sullivan and Babs Smith of The Strategic Coach® for the clarity and tools to achieve my life's vision.

Contents

Acknowledgments

A big heartfelt thank you to my high school chemistry teacher, Frank Siracusa, who took the time to care. Without his caring, I would not have the education I have today. Read more about Mr. Siracusa starting on page 13.

Huge thanks to Dan Sullivan and Babs Smith of The Strategic Coach®. They gave me the clarity and tools to acquire freedom from the frustrations in my life, and to acquire freedom to achieve the vision I have for the rest of my life.

Thank you to the people involved in the publication of this book. Without your help, it would not have been possible. Ross Slater, Jennifer Tribe, and Carissa Stewart of Highspot Inc. provided editorial and publishing guidance that made this book a reality. Liz Cappa, Sandi Serow, and Christina Saburro of R. W. Rogé & Company, Inc. handled all of the administrative work involved in getting it into print. Sally Allen co-authored the Right Sizing chapter with Rosanne Rogé, and Christine Parisi and Jeff Roberto made valuable contributions to The 22-Year Car Loan (see page 51).

And thank you to Tamara Talbot, for her wonderful design work on the book cover.

A Very Special Thank You to My Co-Authors
Steven Rogé is the best son and business partner a dad could ever dream of having. His love and counsel have been influential and invaluable to me.

My wife, and the love of my life, Rosanne Rogé, is the ultimate loving caretaker and the perfect partner in life and in business. She showed me how to take the time to relax, remove my shoes, feel the grass beneath my feet, and enjoy the day. Most importantly, she demonstrates every day that the word "love" is indeed a verb.

Foreword

Ron Rogé could be the poster boy for independent financial advice. In case you've been living on the moon—or in New York City, which tends to be overshadowed by Wall Street's marketing mavens—let me tell you: independent advice is a very good thing. I've been covering independent advisors since 1984, and that experience has given me great respect for these professionals. Like Ron, virtually all of them could have made a lot more money as stockbrokers or insurance agents, but they chose independence in order to better serve their clients.

As the public gradually became aware they had an alternative to in-house financial salespeople, independent advisors—including Ron—became more successful. So much so that today even the *least* independent stockbroker prefers to call him- or herself a "financial advisor." It's one of the great untold American success stories: How a small group of dedicated professionals intent on doing the right thing changed the face of financial advice and, along the way, attained a measure of success they never imagined.

Ron was one of the leaders of that group, which back in the mid-1980s originally numbered fewer than 100 people. They called themselves the National Association of Personal Financial Advisors (NAPFA), and believed their profession should put clients' interests first, free from the economic pressures of buying and selling financial products. In exchange for their advice they charged fees directly to their clients rather than taking sales commissions from brokerage firms or insurance companies.

Ron was chosen to head up the public relations efforts of this "fee-only" movement, largely, I've always suspected, because he was the only board member who lived in proximity to the influential financial magazines, newspapers, and networks in New York City. Through the late 1980s and early 1990s, Ron became a one-man publicity campaign whose goal was to promote the benefits of fee-only, independent financial advice to the public through the media.

At first, Ron's reception at many financial publications was chilly, to say the least. Reporters and the public alike were brainwashed to believe that the only serious financial advice came from Wall Street. Slowly, however, the idea of independent advice and fees paid directly by clients began to sink in. More and more journalists and editors "got it," writing stories about independent advice; perhaps more important, they began more frequently to quote independent advisors as objective experts.

Ron's watershed day—and that of the independent advisory movement— came on September 30, 1996, when Merrill Lynch announced it was moving its 15,000 or so retail brokers away from commissions to fee compensation. Merrill's television ads stated, "No commissions on transactions for a wide variety of investments, including stocks, bonds, and mutual funds." A small but growing band of client-oriented advisors—led by Ron and others—had made independent advice so popular that giant Merrill Lynch, along with the rest of Wall Street, radically changed the way it did business in an effort to keep up. (Of course, no matter what they claim to do on Wall Street, advice given by employee brokers isn't, by NAPFA standards, truly independent. That's made clear by the snowballing success of Ron and other independent advisors, and by Wall Street's continuing efforts to respond to them.)

I first met Ron at NAPFA's 1993 national convention in San Francisco, while he was in the middle of his media blitz. I was a senior editor on the team that had recently launched *Worth* magazine, and I'm sure Ron was schmoozing me just like he was all the other journalists. Yet, after just a few minutes of conversation, I realized that Ron was not only extraordinarily interested in his clients' well-being but also knowledgeable on a broad range of subjects far beyond finance. He also had a charming wit that often contained a deep underlying wisdom.

That day was warm and sunny, so Ron and I played hooky from the confer- ence. After a great lunch in a wharf-side restaurant, we explored the marina district and watched the seals on the docks, and talking like we were old friends. I'm glad to say, we've been friends ever since. Professionally, I've followed Ron's career as he grew his advisory practice into one of the most successful in the industry, all the while exhibiting the objectivity, client orientation, and independence of the best of financial advisors.

Ron has stayed on the cutting edge of independent advice with innovations such as seeking out smaller, "undiscovered" fund managers; designing programs to service smaller clients' goals; networking with other advisors to share their collective experience and wisdom; and, most recently, creating his own fund of mutual funds to lower client costs and adding stock analysis (via his son, Steve) to increase the upside potential of the portfolios they manage.

The Banker and the Fisherman collects the wisdom Ron has gained in his 22 years as a professional advisor, working with clients from all walks of life and observing the markets and the financial services industry. It's not your typical personal finance book, yet both financial consumers and financial professionals will benefit greatly from reading it. Concerned as much with "why" we need to take control of our financial lives as "how" to do it, Ron tackles the tough issues of why Americans don't save more money or even take a greater role in planning for their financial futures. The insights he offers come from a diverse and surprising array of sources, including Viktor E. Frankl's *Man's Search for Meaning*, Warren Buffett, and the US Marines.

Ron's answer to why we don't sock away more, even though a bunch of us are rapidly approaching retirement age, lies uptown from the wire houses, up on Madison Avenue. "Without even realizing it," he writes, "most of us have allowed the great American marketing machine to tell us what we need, when we need it." Today's advertising is so good at convincing us to buy things that there is little left over for our piggy banks. Ron has come to realize that we need to hearken back to our core beliefs if we ever hope to stop listening to advertising's siren lures and use our financial resources to take care of ourselves and the people around us.

In his own down-to-earth style, Ron gently but powerfully shows us how to take control of our lives and our finances. He does so by relating his experiences and observations of some of the brightest minds in finance, the people who helped shape his life, and what's worked for his clients. *The Banker and the Fisherman* is a road map for true financial success, including discussions of how each of us defines "success" and how to create a plan to get there. Along the way, Ron shows us how to leave a legacy, prepare for our retirement, and overcome disastrous knee-jerk investment decisions. Of his Ten Commandments of Investing, my favorites are number 7: "Thou shalt not invest in companies without earnings," and number 10: "Thou shalt not seek stock recommendations from neighbors, friends, or brothers-in-law."

Most important of all, Ron tells us how to live simpler, more meaningful lives—despite what the advertisers tell us we need to have. This remarkable book is about deciding what we really want *before* we waste a lot of time and effort pursuing something meaningless. It's a book about understanding our lives, our culture, and the financial services industry, and about how we can find meaning and attain happiness in the midst of it all.

The wisdom in *The Banker and the Fisherman* springs from a perspective that is truly independent of Wall Street and Madison Avenue and all the pressures— real or imagined—that life today imposes on us. I hope you enjoy Ron's excellent counsel and benefit from it as much as I have.

Bob Clark
Contributing Editor, *Investment Advisor*
Former Editor, *Worth*

Preface

You will probably spend a century on this planet.

One hundred years of life to live. Excellent medical care has become the norm in the United States. That, combined with a bit of luck, is going to make living for a century—or longer—more common. In that time, you will have unique roles to play, special events to plan and attend, and individual responsibilities to fulfill. There will also come a time when the end of life resembles its beginnings, when you will need support and care from others. This need not be a helpless stage. With careful long-term planning, you can ensure that your wishes will be respected and that your foresight will protect your quality of life.

There have been and will be goals to achieve, futures to plan, gifts to give, and legacies to design. Each of these tasks will require you to engage in meaningful dialogue with your wealth management team. Each of these life stages, and the concepts associated with them, is outlined in this book. But this is not a course in economic theory; there is no beginning and no end. Take a look at the table of contents and choose any title you are in the mood to read at a given moment. At whatever page you choose to begin reading, that's the right page. Financial planning works on the same principle. Whenever you choose to begin, that's the right time.

And there are plenty of reasons to create new beginnings. We've structured The Banker and the Fisherman in five sections that mirror five phases of life and five aspects of planning. The book opens with the essential life lessons that continue to guide and inspire our work. Each of the six chapters in this section is meant to encourage you to think about your own influences and your priorities as you work toward your goals. We then move on to advice about financing your home and saving for your children's education, followed by a discussion of investment strategies and tools. Retirement income, issues concerning long-term care, and estate planning wrap up the book.

While researching and writing about each of these topics, we've learned lessons from bankers, fishermen, rabbis, parents, high-school teachers, old friends, and clients like you. The book's title—*The Banker and the Fisherman*—reflects the diversity of those who have taught us and how humbled we have been by the privilege of learning.

Each chapter in the book's five sections originally appeared in our newsletter, *The Rogé Report*. They do not, however, appear here in their original forms. We've restructured, refreshed, and updated them to enhance their longevity and usefulness as you make some of the most important decisions of your life.

Many people would insist that the last sentence of the preceding paragraph should read "the most important *financial* decisions of your life." Too often, people ignore their finances. They hide their ignorance about how the markets, funds, and other investment tools work under a complete indifference to money matters. That's one way that many people fail to see how their expectations for the future, and their behavior in the present, are connected.

We really do live in an era when most people know the price of everything and the value of nothing. This book is our contribution toward reversing that condition. It is a book written by a team of financial planners and wealth managers, but it's not about money. It is about human behavior—both our behavior as individuals and how we act as societies.

If we want to plant the seeds of behaviors and habits that grow success, then we must prepare the soil and create the right conditions. If you're reading this book, it is because you have decided to plant the seeds of a positive future for yourself and, perhaps, those you love. We hope *The Banker and the Fisherman* will help you visualize and realize the garden of your life's dreams. We hope it will support you all the way from initial planting to final harvest. We hope it will help you grow the garden of the century.

1 | The Meaning of Life

1.1

The Banker and the Fisherman

The following story shows how differently two people and two cultures can view life and retirement. The original author is unknown.

An American investment banker was standing on the pier in a small Mexican village when a tiny boat carrying one fisherman docked. Inside the boat were several large yellowfin tuna. The American complimented the fisherman on the quality of his fish and asked how long it had taken to catch them. The fisherman replied, "Only a little while."

The banker then asked the fisherman why he hadn't stayed out longer to catch more fish. The fisherman said he had caught enough to support his family's immediate needs.

The banker shot back, "But what do you do with the rest of your time?"

The fisherman replied, "I sleep late, fish a little, play with my children, take a siesta with my wife, and stroll into the village each evening, where I sip wine and play guitar with my amigos. I have a full and busy life."

The banker scoffed, "I have an MBA from Harvard, and I can help you. You should spend more time fishing and, with the proceeds, buy a bigger boat. With the proceeds from the bigger boat, you could buy several boats, and eventually you would have a fleet. Instead of selling your catch to a middleman, you could sell directly to the processor, eventually opening your own cannery. You would control the product, processing, and distribution. You could leave this small coastal fishing village and move to Mexico City, then Los Angeles, and eventually New York, where you would run your expanding enterprise."

The fisherman asked, "How long will all this take?"

"Fifteen to 20 years," answered the banker.

In order to make the most of your money, you need to know where you want to go and determine the best way to get there.

"But what then?"

The banker laughed and said, "That's the best part. When the time is right you would announce an Initial Public Offering and sell your company stock to the public and become very rich. You would make millions."

"Millions. Then what?"

The banker replied, "Then you would retire and move to a small coastal fishing village where you would sleep late, fish a little, play with your kids, take a siesta with your wife, and stroll into the village in the evenings, where you could sip wine and play guitar with your amigos."

As you can see from this short story, most people view things differently, and even an educated investment banker can miss the point. You may already have much of what you are looking for, but just don't realize it. In order to make the most of your money and your life, you need to know where you want to go and then determine the best way to get there. Our hope is that this story and the book will help you on your journey.

1.2

The Pursuit of Happiness
Ronald W. Rogé

According to the *Merriam-Webster Dictionary*, happiness is "a state of well-being and contentment; a pleasurable or satisfying experience." Nowhere does the definition mention money. Yet we continue to hear people associating happiness with money. We hear them say, "When I win the lottery ..." and "When I achieve a certain balance in my account ... I'll be happy."

There's no question that winning the lottery would be an exciting experience. There's fun in pondering what might be done with all that money. And freedom, too, because you're able to think beyond your present circumstances to ponder new possibilities and opportunities. But the reality isn't as rosy: in the United States, you must pay almost half of your winnings in income tax[1] and then figure out a way to shelter the remaining portion of your good fortune from estate taxes. Then there are all those relatives and friends looking for a handout; and perhaps you'd like to give a portion of your windfall to a charity or two. Having money can complicate your life. Money can also disappear quickly, along with the initial elation of instant riches.

---

1. In the US approximately 35% of lottery winnings must be paid in federal taxes and between 6% and 8% must be paid in state taxes.

According to a 2006 article in London's *Financial Times*, "Random samples of citizens today report the same degree of psychological well-being and satisfaction with their lives as did their (poorer) parents. In the US, happiness has fallen over time. White American females are markedly less happy than were their mothers." The article goes on to say, "In the US, even though real incomes have risen sixfold, the per-capita suicide rate is the same as in the year 1900."

Grandma said that money wouldn't bring you happiness.

The article's author, Andrew Oswald, a professor of economics at the University of Warwick, has conducted extensive research that undermines the supposed link between economic growth and happiness. In the *Financial Times* piece, he points out that even as our wealth grows, happiness remains elusive because we are creatures of comparison: "Research last year showed that happiness levels depend inversely on the earnings levels of a person's neighbors. Prosperity next door makes you dissatisfied. It is relative income that matters: when everyone in society gets wealthier, average well-being stays the same."

Another reason Americans don't become happier is habituation. Experiences wear off. Some researchers believe that after a pay raise people get used to their greater income and eventually return to their original happy or unhappy states. As Oswald concludes, "Human beings are bad at forecasting what will make them happy. People systematically choose the wrong things for themselves."

Grandma said that money wouldn't bring you happiness. She was right, but she should have added the qualifier "for very long." If you didn't believe your grandma, well, now you have some studies to back up what she knew all along.

It's true that money is a great facilitator. It can give you a more comfortable lifestyle. It allows you to create the environment in which you want to live. It permits access to services and people that can make your life more comfortable. But it can't create happiness for very long.

So if money isn't happiness, what is? And how do you achieve well-being and contentment? Writing in *USA Today* in 2006, Sharon Jayson quotes Jonathan Haidt, associate professor of psychology at the University of Virginia and author of the book *The Happiness Hypothesis*, on the determinants of happiness:

> Happiness has a very weak relation to events in our lives. Your happiness level is determined mostly by the structure in your brain—not by whether good or bad things happen to you. Negative events hurt or feel bad, but they are not usually as bad as we think and don't last as long as we think. Happiness is an individual thing, like a thermostat in our brains with a baseline that's predetermined by genetics. We all move, up or down, around our set point, depending on life events. The key to the psychology of happiness is to move to the upper range of your potential.

Antidepressants are a wonderful pharmaceutical for seriously ill individuals. However, the sale of antidepressants has become a huge business for the pharmaceutical industry because people are requesting them in an effort to move to the upper range of their potential by taking pills. They believe that if they get there, they will be happy.

I decided to write this chapter because, as a financial advisor for more than 20 years, I've had the privilege of working with hundreds of families and individuals in creating the paths that lead to their futures. People I worked with 20 years ago are experiencing that future today. These experiences have given me insights that no amount of generic research can duplicate. So, the purpose of this chapter is to share with you what I've learned in helping clients move to the upper limits of their happiness potential.

It all starts when we're born. We come into this world naked, needing a roof over our heads, clothes on our backs, and food to nourish our growth. From day one, our parents try to fulfill our most basic needs, which psychologist Abraham Maslow represented in his famous tiered triangle. Once we achieve one level, we move up and try to achieve the next. And if, at some future point, a deficiency is detected at a lower level, we act quickly to go back and remove that deficiency before ascending the ladder again.

While Maslow's original triangle was composed of five levels or stages, it has since been revamped to include eight:

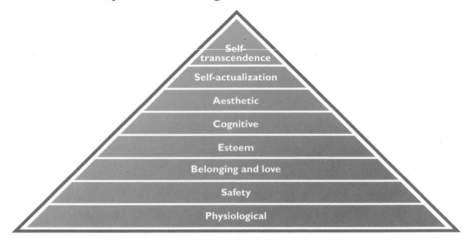

1. **Physiological:** These needs relate to the basics of staying alive, such as finding food and shelter. Information that is not directly connected to helping a person meet these needs is left unattended.
2. **Safety:** These needs help us avoid danger.
3. **Belonging and love:** These needs address our connections to others. They are what inspire us to marry, have families, and be part of communities.
4. **Esteem:** These needs involve seeking and gaining approval and recognition. At this level, people try to develop their egos in order to gain self-respect and the respect of others.
5. **Cognitive:** These are the needs people have to know, understand, and explore the world around them.
6. **Aesthetic:** These needs produce symmetry, order, and beauty.
7. **Self-actualization:** These needs involve self-fulfillment and realizing one's potential.
8. **Self-transcendence:** This is the need to connect to something beyond the ego and, therefore, help others find self-fulfillment and realize their own potential.

People in the growth levels of cognitive needs, aesthetic needs, and self-actualization seek edifying information. They seek information on how to connect to something beyond themselves, or to show others how to connect.

I know people who have never gone beyond levels three or four, and yet they seem to be very happy. And I've helped clients over the years who were well beyond level four and were very unhappy. After going through the goal-setting and planning process, they discovered their lives were too complex. My team and I helped them create a simpler lifestyle. We did that by first interpreting and then simplifying their lives through a process of self-discovery. The result? Those clients reported a welcome sense of relief, based in part on being more aware and in control of their affairs.

After the events of September 11, 2001, many people who were not directly affected by the terrorist attacks felt vulnerable. For them, there was a deficiency in level two of Maslow's hierarchy of needs. People's sense of security was taken away. They could not function beyond level two for a while because they needed reassurance that measures were being taken to keep them safe. As time passed without further attacks, they gradually felt more secure and began moving up the ladder again.

Money can help us climb Maslow's hierarchy of needs. Even with money, however, unexpected events can quickly move us down the ladder as we seek to repair a vulnerability or two. In that sense, the happiness that money brings is always conditional and tentative.

Maybe Aristotle got it right when he claimed that happiness "cannot be achieved in less than a full lifetime. One swallow does not make a summer; neither does one fine day. And, one day, or indeed any brief period of felicity, does not make man entirely and perfectly happy."

One of the best books I ever read was *Man's Search for Meaning* by Viktor E. Frankl, a psychiatrist who struggled for survival during three years in Auschwitz and other Nazi concentration camps. Rather than dwell on the great horrors he experienced and observed, Frankl focused on the hard fight for daily survival he and his fellow prisoners waged. He realized that, as a psychiatrist, he had the opportunity to observe humanity at its worst. He had a real-life laboratory in which to study why some people gave up while others survived. Frankl's conclusion was that life's basic motivation is "the will to meaning." Or, as the philosopher Friedrich Nietzsche put it, "He who has a why to live for can bear almost any how."

Frankl's sage words are worth pausing over:

> The meaning of life differs from man to man, from day to day and from hour to hour. What matters, therefore, is not the meaning of life in general ... but rather the specific meaning of a person's life at a given moment. ... Everyone has his own specific vocation or mission in life to carry out a concrete assignment which demands fulfillment. Therein he cannot be replaced, nor can his life be repeated. Thus, everyone's task is as unique as is his specific opportunity to implement it.

If you live simply, you won't be as anxious about the unimportant things in life.

Okay, so problems are presented in life and it's up to us to solve them. Is happiness the ability to solve problems? Perhaps. Frankl suggested that in order to have a meaningful life we need a greater purpose than ourselves. We need something to do, someone to love. We may also find it in suffering. Strangely enough, suffering is the source of creativity.

I've observed over the years that clients who suffer from life-threatening diseases or the death of their spouses or children often gain clarity about their purpose in life. When we suffer, the meaning and purpose of our existence is clarified. It's what gives us the strength to carry on under great adversity.

Frankl observed that men who had lost purpose in their lives would give up and die in the camps. This fact became so apparent that it got to the point that Frankl and his fellow prisoners could predict such people's deaths within days. Those who, like himself, had a greater purpose in life, even if they were sometimes in worse physical condition than those who had died, somehow endured.

A friend sent me an e-mail recently that ended with five rules for a happy life:

1. Free your heart from hatred.
2. Live simply.
3. Free your mind from worries.
4. Give more.
5. Expect less.

I like these rules. Think about it. If you have hatred in your heart, you can't be happy. If you live simply, you won't be as anxious about the unimportant things in life. If you worry all the time, you can't function or focus. If you give more of yourself to others, you'll feel good. If you expect less, you won't be disappointed.

My experience has led me to conclude that happiness begins when you learn to like yourself. We all know a few unhappy people. It seems to me they don't like themselves and complain about everything. They complain because they're trying to blame their unhappiness on others instead of attempting to learn their greater purpose. As my friend Sherry Cross likes to say, "They are not happy in their own skin."

If you, however, understand your greater purpose and try to observe the five rules, you may well be on your way to happiness.

1.3

Thank You, Mr. Siracusa
Ronald W. Rogé

I'm not one to dwell much on my past. On the contrary, I've been described as barely living in the present and mostly thinking of the future, a character trait that likely reflects my training as a financial planner and investment advisor. In this profession, it's mostly about the future.

Even though I rarely think about yesterday, I've learned from my personal coach, Dan Sullivan of The Strategic Coach® Program that, from time to time, it's helpful to ask, "What am I grateful for?" It's an exercise Dan calls Gratitude Focus™ and the way it works is simple. You give yourself three minutes to write down everything you're grateful for in life. It's a wonderful exercise if you're feeling down because it creates a positive attitude as soon as you do it.

I've been doing the Gratitude Focus™ for about eight years now and have come to appreciate the choices I've made during my lifetime. After all, these choices have helped me get to where I am today.

Believe it or not, the word *decide* is related to the word *homicide*. Both have the same root, which means to cut or kill. When you come to a fork in the road you must decide which direction to take, eliminating the other option. Consider, for example, my decision to join the United States Naval Air Reserve rather than be drafted into the army during the Vietnam War. Instead of just being an army foot soldier, it occurred to me that perhaps I could acquire a marketable skill in the navy before being sent into harm's way. If I survived, I would at least have practical training as a pilot or navigator that I could parlay into a job following my stint in the armed forces.

I tried to persuade my friends Gary and Billy to go with me to be tested for the Naval Air Reserve. They chose not to because they felt it was too much effort. I remember them saying they would just let the army draft them, serve their two years, and get it over with. I even remember—as if it were yesterday— where that conversation took place, because their response seemed so odd to me.

Our birthdays were two months apart, so at age 18 we were called for our pre-induction physicals on the same day. That meant Gary, Billy, and I were about to be drafted into the army and sent to the jungles of South Vietnam. As planned, I joined the Naval Air Reserve and was lucky enough to serve my active duty stateside during the war. Both Gary and Billy were drafted into the army, went to boot camp, and were sent overseas together (although they served in different units).

Gary was severely wounded about a month before he was expected to come home. His wounds were so bad that he has not been able to work since returning from Vietnam. Billy was killed in action two weeks before his tour of duty was scheduled to end. I remember it took about two weeks for his body to be returned home. Billy's name is on the Vietnam Veterans Memorial in Washington, DC, along with the names of 60,000 other military personnel who gave their lives in service to their country. To this day, 40 years later, I still cry when I visit that memorial.

Our past is clearly defined by the choices we make along the way. It reminds me of something Woody Allen once said: "More than any other time in history, mankind faces a crossroads. One path leads to despair and utter hopelessness; the other, to total extinction. Let us pray we have the wisdom to choose correctly."

Having choices is good for most people, even if not for Woody Allen. However, because we grow up inside the worlds our families create for us, we sometimes aren't aware of the alternatives. We rarely look past what we know.

That was certainly the case with me. No one in my family had ever gone beyond high school. College was not a word in my vocabulary—at least not until I met Mr. Siracusa. When I knew Frank Siracusa he was a 25-year-old Columbia University graduate who, in 1963, was teaching chemistry at Franklin K. Lane High School in Brooklyn, New York. One day, Mr. Siracusa asked me to stay after class. He took me aside and said, "Ron, you seem to like chemistry. What are your plans after you graduate?" Up to that point in my life no one had ever asked me that question. Quite frankly, I had never thought about it. I just didn't realize I could choose the future I wanted for myself.

Mr. Siracusa suggested I consider going to college. "Do you think you might like to work as a chemist?" he asked me. I replied, "Yes." After all, I liked chemistry. Not only did Mr. Siracusa point me toward chemistry, but he also sensed I would need some active guidance to help me get into college. This is an important point, because he took the time to call a friend of his who was the head of the Department of Chemistry at Bronx Community College, and told him he was sending me along to be interviewed for admission.

Our past is clearly defined by the choices we make along the way.

I took the "A" train to the Bronx, application in hand. At the interview, Mr. David Gorman said, "I see you live in Brooklyn. New York City Community College in downtown Brooklyn has the same program. That would be a much shorter commute for you." He then called the head of its chemistry department and said he was sending me over for an interview. The rest, as they say, is history. I got my associate's degree in chemistry from New York City Community College, a bachelor's degree in chemistry from Long Island University, and a master of science degree from Polytechnic University in Brooklyn.

I have learned several lessons from this re-examination of my past and the choices I've made:

- It doesn't take much effort or time to have a dramatic impact on someone's life.
- It's gratifying to help others realize their objectives and to make a meaningful difference in their lives.
- When you suggest to others they have a choice, especially when they may not know they have one, recognize that you may have to show them how to do what you are suggesting.
- Don't dwell on decisions you regret; move forward by creating your own future. You can't do anything about the past. Dan Sullivan says, "Forgiveness is when you give up the hope of having a better past."

Are you working every day to achieve the kind of future you have in mind? We can't do anything about the past, but we can work toward the future we want by knowing the choices we have. Acting on those choices is what leads us in the desired direction. As Sullivan also likes to say, "The future is your property."

When I meet with clients, I always spend time discussing the future they want. When we start the conversation they usually don't know how to get where they want to be for one or more of the following reasons:

1. They have too much information and are confused about their options.
2. They may not be aware of the choices they have because they are too close to the situation.
3. They don't know how to work the numbers for the plan they are contemplating.

4.   They are not sure how to handle the uncertainties and risks that are always present in planning for the future.

Mr. Siracusa taught me well—not just about chemistry, but about life, the choices we have, and how to move forward and achieve long-term goals. So, thank you, Mr. Siracusa, for caring and making me aware that I had a choice and that I could be the architect of my own future. And thank you for showing me how to get there, too.

Postscript: *After 43 years of not having seen or heard from him, I recently managed to contact Mr. Siracusa to thank him personally for the impact he had on my life. He and I, along with my good friend from high school, Jack Muhlstein, had a delightful lunch that lasted more than four hours.*

1.4

What's Important ... and What's Not
Ronald W. Rogé

I was sitting in the waiting room of my allergist's office and couldn't help but overhear his administrative staffers, who were talking rather loudly. One employee shouted to the other, "Hey, guess what? My 18-year-old son just got a job. And he makes more than you do—$11 per hour."

> We Americans have created such a consumer culture that we don't know the value of the things that really matter.

While not particularly interesting to me, I thought it was odd that all three middle-aged female employees seemed to know precisely what each other's hourly wages were. Then the conversation turned to Prada bags. One woman said, "I just got a knockoff Prada bag for $65." One of the other women responded that her husband had bought her a knockoff Louis Vuitton pocketbook for $50, while the real one cost $215.

As I thought about the conversations on my drive home, it occurred to me that we Americans have created such a consumer culture that we don't know the value of the things that really matter. We seem to know the price of everything and the value of nothing.

I was reminded of a book I read a few years ago, Beppe Severgnini's *Ciao, America: An Italian Discovers the U.S.* Severgnini is one of Italy's favorite authors, and he spent a year living among and observing Americans in Washington, DC. Two of the observations he made relate to the story I'm telling here:

1. Americans are obsessed with competition.
2. Americans are obsessed with numbers and codes (e.g., social security numbers, personal identification numbers, e-mail addresses, credit cards, checking account numbers, debit cards).

The marketers behind Prada and Louis Vuitton have obviously convinced the women who work in my allergist's office that their pocketbooks are the best. And, as the story shows, those women knew the prices of both the real and knockoff versions.

To show just how clueless I am, I didn't know Prada makes pocketbooks. I knew only that Prada is a high-end shoe manufacturer. I was aware that Louis Vuitton makes pocketbooks, but I didn't know (and still don't) whether it produces shoes. Knowing whether or not Louis Vuitton makes shoes will not affect my life 25 years from now; therefore, that bit of information is not important to me, What I believe is more important for me, and for most Americans, is knowing what it will cost to live the life one wants and how to acquire the funds necessary to achieve that goal. I'm talking here about the potential costs of:

- Retirement
- College education for children and/or grandchildren
- Buying a home
- Caring for aging parents
- Caring for a dependent adult child
- Establishing an emergency fund
- Protecting loved ones against risks (e.g., death or disability of the breadwinner, need for a nursing home)
- Leaving loved ones an inheritance
- Making the world a better place in which to live

On my drive home after my allergist appointment I asked myself the question, "Do most Americans know what it will take to achieve these goals, and, if not, why not?" After all, most of us are very good with numbers, and we seem to know what's good quality, along with the price we'll have to pay for it.

My conclusion—based on anecdotal evidence, research papers I've read on the subject, and my experience as a certified financial planner—is a resounding no! We don't have a clue. I believe the reason we don't have a clue is that marketers distract us with unimportant things, so much so that we fail to focus on what is important.

So what can we do about it? If we could get marketers to focus their messages on "the important stuff of life" (to paraphrase the late scientific author, educator, and astronomer, Carl Sagan), we would be discussing the numbers necessary to achieve the goals for our life journeys, rather than the price of Prada bags. The government could help, as well. Perhaps taxing unsolicited marketing material and giving tax credits to marketing firms that create public service messages about what it takes to achieve one's goals would begin to shift our focus toward what is truly important.

The next time you're attracted to a marketing message, stop and ask yourself, "How does knowing this information relate to my top three life goals?" If it doesn't, turn away and enjoy the journey toward obtaining "the important stuff of life."

1.5

The Movie Star and the Rabbi
Ronald W. Rogé

Sometimes we don't see the value of setting goals until we see a goal-setter become successful. Arnold Schwarzenegger is an example of someone who set a goal and worked tenaciously to reach it.

Schwarzenegger came to the United States from Austria at the age of 21, with just $20 in his pocket. Among his many achievements are the Mr. Universe, Mr. Olympia, and Mr. World bodybuilding titles. Not too many people know, however, that in addition to starting and running a bricklaying and masonry business with a partner, and running a bodybuilding supplies mail-order company, Schwarzenegger obtained a business degree from the University of Wisconsin and then launched a successful real estate enterprise. He then moved on to movies, where he became one of the biggest action heroes Hollywood has ever seen. After getting involved in politics, he set his sights on the governorship of California and won the election.

While some folks might say, "Wow, Schwarzenegger was lucky," I wouldn't. Behind that supposed luck was the ability to see the future, and then muster the energy to build it. Like me, you've probably often heard the expression, "Luck is the residue of design," a saying that's attributed to everyone from

John Milton to Vince Lombardi. Even if we don't agree with his political views, we have to admire Schwarzenegger's ability to visualize his goals and his determination to achieve them. What are your visions for the future?

Several years ago, I attended a planners conference where the speaker was a well-known rabbi who specialized in counseling the sick and dying, as well as survivors of traumatic experiences. He discussed how most people go through life without setting goals because they believe they will live forever. They procrastinate about figuring out what they want to achieve. An interesting and true observation, but nothing I hadn't heard before.

Then the rabbi got everyone's attention by asking us to complete a little exercise. He asked us to draw a horizontal line across a piece of paper. At the left end of the line he had us write the letter B and, at the right end, the letter D. He then said, "This is a visual of your life. The B is when you were born and the D is your death."

> *Most people go through life without setting goals because they believe they will live forever.*

"Now," he said, "put an X on the line where you think you are today. Between the X and the D is the rest of your life. What do you want it to be like? What do you want to achieve? Whom do you want to help? Where do you want to go?"

B ——————— THE PAST ——————— **X** ——————— THE REST OF YOUR LIFE ——————— **D**

That rabbi certainly got everyone in the room thinking. For the remaining days of the conference we all talked about the exercise and how instructive and motivating it had been.

The rabbi also shared his experience with counseling the dying. He had never heard a dying person who wished for more hours spent in the office. Regrets were always about not having achieved goals that had never been articulated, goals such as spending more time with family and friends, traveling to places around the world, and trying new things.

So, while you may feel that folks like Arnold Schwarzenegger are just lucky, think again. Visualizing the future and defining goals are the first steps toward constructing the rest of your life.

1.6

What Is Your Legacy?

Ronald W. Rogé

If you would know the road ahead, ask someone who has traveled it.

—Chinese proverb

I have been in business for over 20 years. During that time, I've noticed a growing trend among parents and grandparents to want to leave something valuable to their progeny.

A legacy can take many forms, the most common of which is assets, bequeathed either directly or through a will. But it might be better to consider passing on something that may ultimately prove even more valuable than money: a summary of life lessons learned. Indeed, the proliferation of courses offered in colleges and on the Internet about how to compose memoirs and autobiographies reflects the growing popularity of such testaments.

Perhaps because they are consumed by the complicated and demanding business of life, most people depart this world without leaving much of a record of their time. I recently bought an old stock certificate for my son, Steven. The Chemical National Bank of New York had issued it on February 16, 1875, to James Lenox Banks, MD. Out of curiosity I ran a quick Internet search to see if I could learn something about this one-time investor. Though much was written about his son (James Lenox Banks, Jr.) and the family's later connection through marriage to the Astors, little was available on James Senior.

Success in life creates legacies, but money is only part of the larger picture.

Just the opposite is true for President Gerald R. Ford, who passed away at the age of 93. Do a Google search and you'll find hundreds of thousands of pages about his life and legacy. While most of us are not famous like President Ford, we can still leave an account of our lives for the benefit of posterity. In fact, many people today are deciding they want to tell their stories. They want to explain how they prospered, to share their beliefs, and to describe how they fit into the larger events of their times.

In the movie *Anger Management*, Jack Nicholson's character keeps asking Adam Sandler's character who he is, because Sandler is having difficulty explaining himself. It's an excellent question. Think about it. Who are you?

A memoir is an effective way of communicating who you are and what your life is all about to your children and grandchildren and, eventually, their children. As a possible first step you could get in touch with a professional writer and editor. Following an established interview-based format, you could create a biographical summary that would become a personal component of your estate.

Success in life creates legacies, but money is only part of the larger picture. Money, in fact, may not be the most important part of your legacy. Share your unique experiences with future generations. It's easier than you think.

 2 | **Planning, Saving, and Security**

2.1

Saving Up Instead of Catching Up
Ronald W. Rogé

A reporter called me recently to ask why most Americans can't seem to save for the future. That conversation got me thinking more about why most people can't—or won't—save.

The United States has long had the developed world's lowest rate of savings. Recent federal government statistics indicate that the national savings rate is now negative, meaning that the average consumer spends more on goods and services than he or she takes home in after-tax income. We are, indeed, a nation of debtors. This disturbing phenomenon may have a troubling impact on both the nation's economy and—on a more personal level—the quality of retirement for millions of people.

Most Americans are caught in a vicious cycle of relying on credit to buy things while trying to pay off those bills and continuing to use credit to buy even more things. The cycle looks something like this:

The United States has long had the developed world's lowest rate of savings.

- **January to March:** Pay off bills from holiday shopping.
- **March to April:** Pay off winter vacation bills.
- **April to May:** Pay unexpected tax bills.
- **June:** Pay opening-the-pool and landscaping expenses after winter.
- **July to August:** Enjoy vacation with the kids.
- **September:** Pay off debts accumulated over the summer.
- **October to November:** Pay off back-to-school expenses.
- **November to December:** Accumulate holiday shopping debts to be paid off in the first three months of the new year.

Then there are those other expenses that need to be saved for, such as Grandma's 90th birthday party, home repairs, or a child's wedding. Most people have every intention of saving for those kind of major events, but somehow time flies by and not one single dime has been squirreled away. I could ask why, but I know the answer: all those people are hoping. But hoping for what? Well, probably to win the lottery.

So the vicious cycle starts over again. And it never ends unless steps are taken to stop it.

On top of the spending and catch-up cycle, there are taxes to consider. From 10% to 35% of your hard-earned salary is lost to federal income and Federal Insurance Contributions Act (FICA) taxes. A further 4% to 8% goes to state and local levies. In other words, far more than a third—closer to 40%—of each workday is devoted to satisfying your tax obligations.

A famous definition of insanity is "repeating the same thing over and over yet expecting a different result each time." So how can you stop the insanity?

Here are four steps that will get you headed toward success:

1. Begin tracking your expenses on a daily basis.

2. Prepare a realistic budget for the next 12 months that includes:
   - Savings in your budget as an expense against your income
   - Your taxes as a budget expense

3. Accelerate your progress by automation. Don't trust yourself to save. Set it up to be done automatically for several different accounts:
   - Retirement
   - Children's education
   - Emergency fund
   - Vacation fund

4. Get a 15-year mortgage instead of the conventional 30-year type. You'll be amazed at how quickly you can build up principal in your home and pay down the debt. Accelerating your mortgage schedule is an effective and painless way to save without realizing you're actually saving.

Following these steps will help switch off the counterproductive behavior that got you into the vicious cycle, and will once again put you in control of your financial destiny. In fact, recognizing and admitting that you have lapsed into a dangerous state of financial indiscipline is the first step to recovery and, ultimately, success.

HELPFUL TOOL

To create a budget, go to www.rwroge.com and click on the Financial Planning Tools tab. Then, click on Income and Expenditure Worksheet to download the tool. The worksheet will provide a clear picture of outflows and inflows, the crucial first step to breaking the vicious cycle of catching up instead of saving up.

2.2

Noah's Rule
Ronald W. Rogé

Learning from mistakes creates wisdom. One thing I learned from attending the Berkshire Hathaway annual shareholder meeting in the spring of 2005 was that both Warren Buffett and his partner, Charlie Munger, are still striving to learn and improve. Both men—Warren in his mid-70s and Charlie in his early 80s—were willing to discuss their mistakes and the lessons they had learned from them. During a five-hour question-and-answer session, they seemed to enjoy sharing with the audience the wisdom they had accumulated over the years.

Perhaps the best example of the type of wisdom shared at that meeting came from Buffett. Commenting on the poor performance in 2001 of General Re Corporation, a reinsurance company owned by Berkshire Hathaway, Buffett said he had overlooked or dismissed the possibility of large-scale terrorism losses to the company. He admitted, "I violated Noah's Rule. Predicting rain doesn't count. Building arks does."

To the Warren Buffetts of the world, arks are actions taken to address the risks associated with predictions. Arks demonstrate that a person is prepared to deal with risks should their predictions come true.

Wouldn't it be great if all of the predictions made in the investment media observed Noah's Rule? Sources making predictions should be asked what they're doing in response to their forecasts—for themselves, as well as for their clients. Where are their arks?

The action, or ark, I use at my company is never to put all the money in one basket:

- Always divide money into at least three asset classes (i.e., stocks, bonds, and cash).
- Always remain well diversified within a single asset class.
- Always look for lower-risk, better-return securities.
- Always know your tolerance for risk.
- Always perform in-house research.

As Dan Sullivan of the Strategic Coach® likes to say, "Always make your learning greater than your experience." Buffett and Munger certainly do.

2.3

It's Never a Bad Time to Do the Right Thing

Ronald W. Rogé

In the weeks following the tragic events of September 11, 2001, we received many telephone calls from the media. They tended to ask the same two questions, which we've printed below along with our responses. Our answers were relevant then and, we believe, continue to be important now because there will always be threats or adverse conditions facing investors.

Considering the state of the financial market, what should an investor do?

In our experience, people who ask this question don't have a plan to follow. They have not outlined their goals, time lines, risk tolerance, tax situations, or other criteria that are important when creating a financial plan.

Such people are usually paralyzed because they've discovered that what they did in the past was inappropriate for them and, as a result, they lost money they couldn't afford to lose. They're actually fearful of recognizing their mistakes and correcting them because they're afraid that after they rearrange their finances, their old investments will rally and regain any losses. As a result of their fear, they remain inactive and ride their investments down to zero.

If you have a financial road map to follow during emotional times, you can avoid making similar mistakes. Our advice is that it's never a bad time to do the right thing.

What can a family do when its primary income provider dies?
If a family doesn't take steps beforehand to protect its income and assets in the face of an unforeseen tragedy, there is little it can do after the fact. Grieving the loss of a loved one is difficult enough; it's even more painful for a family that is not financially prepared.

Before anything happens to you or someone in your family, you should do the right thing. As soon as possible, every income provider needs to take the following five steps:

1. Before investing a dime in the market, establish an **emergency fund** that will cover from three to six months of living expenses. The money can be kept in a money market fund with check-writing privileges. If your family's primary income provider becomes disabled or loses his or her life, this account will give you short-term relief from financial worries while you sort through all the necessary paperwork from wills and insurance, the proceeds of which will financially care for you going forward.

2. Buy as much **term life insurance** as those left behind will require. For most families with children, a $2-million policy is a minimum amount. The proceeds from the policy will not only provide future income but will also help pay for the children's college education.

3. Buy a **disability policy** that will cover your primary income provider during periods of disability.

4. Buy **long-term care insurance** for you and your spouse. It will help protect your assets should either of you require skilled nursing home care. You don't need to be over 50 years of age to buy this important coverage.

5. Develop a program to **pay down debt**. Ultimately, you want to be debt free.

Don't let uncertainty breed despair. By taking these five steps you'll provide your family with some peace of mind in the event of unexpected disability, a nursing-home stay, or the death of the primary income provider.

A closing thought about these recommendations is that no stock tip, investment strategy, or fantastic portfolio recommendation will ever be more important to you than the advice we've just given. Don't just think about it. Do it!

If a family doesn't take steps beforehand to protect its income and assets in the face of an unforeseen tragedy, there is little it can do after the fact.

2.4

Your Home Is No Longer Your Savings Account

Ronald W. Rogé

For several decades now, housing prices have appreciated rapidly, primarily because of easy credit policies that have allowed more people to own their own homes. The trend accelerated until problems in the subprime mortgage markets brought the party to an end. But from 1994 to 2005, according to Moody's Economy.com, some 3.2 million people in the United States were able to buy homes thanks to subprime mortgages, thereby making the dream of home ownership a reality for a record number of Americans.

As the housing market gained momentum and lenders loosened mortgage requirements, the homes people built and bought got bigger. Keeping up with the Joneses was another American phenomenon. You watched your neighbor build or move into a bigger home, so naturally you wanted one, as well.

Today, there is a term for these elephantine dwellings: McMansions. "Would you like to supersize that home?" builders regularly ask. Until recently, I thought McMansions were anything over 5,000 square feet, but in the course of a conversation I recently had with a decorator, she mentioned she was working for a client who had just built a 22,000-square-foot extravaganza.

When I asked how many people lived in the home, the decorator said, "Just two," adding that the owners were unsure they would have enough room to do everything they wanted to do. So much for 800-square-foot Levitt and Sons homes built in the 1940s and 1950s here on Long Island, one of the country's original suburbs. Today, those dwellings would be considered merely walk-in closets.

The rapid rise in housing prices over the past few decades has allowed many people, especially baby boomers, to think of their homes as savings accounts. That approach offered a good pretext for rationalizing meager retirement savings or the absence of meaningful financial reserves for college costs. It certainly had worked for their parents, who purchased their modest homes in the 1950s and then sold them at much-appreciated values. Those same parents then used the proceeds to buy less-expensive condos in Florida and deposited the balance into savings accounts or investment portfolios. Their portfolios produced income to supplement payments from pensions and Social Security. In effect, this unexpected appreciation in the value of their homes represented a significant savings, and now the boomers have come to think of the strategy as a permanent fixture on the financial landscape.

> *The basic assumption that a house, or property in general, will always be an appreciating asset seemed to be playing out nicely—until recently.*

The basic assumption that a house, or property in general, will always be an appreciating asset seemed to be playing out nicely—until recently. That's when America's free-wheeling mortgage lenders—giddy from a steady flow of cheap money—were suddenly called to account, sparking a liquidity crisis in the mortgage and mortgage-derivative markets. The extent of the fallout from this latest shock to the real estate markets is uncertain, but it will be significant. That includes a wave of foreclosures that could affect millions of households.

All those houses suddenly coming back onto the market will depress housing prices further, sharply diminishing the piggy-bank effect of home ownership on which boomers have come to count. Also, remember that most boomers do not have the traditional defined-benefit pension plans their parents enjoyed. And Social Security, which already requires boomers to wait longer before collecting full benefits, will not be as generous as it once was.

I believe this credit crisis will be the watershed event that will see a fundamental decline in real estate values that could last for years and maybe even a decade. American families' net worth (i.e., the difference be-

Once Americans realize their wealth is shrinking, they will rediscover the virtues of saving.

tween assets and liabilities) was $10.95 trillion in 1982; it had exploded to $57.7 trillion by the end of 2007. However, the period prior to 1982 (1965 to 1981) was a period of net-worth reduction (wealth destruction) in the US. My point is that history tells us these boom-and-bust cycles happen over many years and are largely unnoticeable to the general public.

In the next economic cycle wealth appreciation will not come from the increase in the value of real estate; it may, however, take most Americans three to five years to realize that fact. The problems in the housing market, together with other factors such as higher energy costs, a weakening job market, and low wage growth, will focus the minds of America's reflexive consumers on the need to save, and save aggressively. In the future, wealth appreciation will come from saving, which is and has been non-existent in this country. In fact, because of high levels of debt, America's collective savings rate was actually negative in 2005 and much of 2006, something that had not been seen since the Great Depression.

Once Americans realize their wealth is shrinking, they will rediscover the virtues of saving, which will require planning, discipline, and, very likely, the need to work much longer than they had anticipated. For many, the task will be daunting.

An increase in consumer savings will lead to a reduction in consumer spending. Consumption as a percentage of our gross domestic product (GDP) has been rising for 20 years. As I noted earlier, our national savings rate has been below zero for some time. When that trend reverses, it will have a detrimental impact on the economy because it will cause a reduction in consumption, which accounts for approximately two-thirds of our GDP.

When a growing number of people decide to work longer, the labor supply increases. If demand for the services this labor pool provides does not increase, lower wages will result—a deflationary phenomenon. Some of this deflation will be offset by the increased demand for labor, providing the geriatric services boomers will need as they age. However, those services will be provided by a younger workforce, composed largely of immigrant labor. In addition, the demand in real estate will be for geriatric care facilities to house the boomers and lower-cost housing for the first generation of new immigrants, who come to the US to provide the services the boomers will demand.

We have already seen this result with the downsizing of corporate America. In the 1990s, many thousands of skilled workers were laid off. Then, after a year of unemployment, they accepted lower-paying jobs. What happened has been termed *creative destruction*, a concept popularized in 1942 by the economist Joseph Schumpeter, who described the process of transformation that accompanies radical innovation. In Schumpeter's vision of capitalism, innovation driven by entrepreneurs is the force that sustains long-term economic growth, even as it destroys the value of established companies that have enjoyed some degree of monopoly power. While creative destruction will always be present, our economy will also have to contend with the reality of a graying workforce and slowing of GDP growth caused by an increase in savings and a decrease in consumption.

Not everything, though, is negative with this scenario. The weaker US dollar will allow us to pay down our deficit more easily with a devalued currency. In addition, increased savings will stoke investment in stocks, bonds, and other assets that promote economic growth. That will increase the value of stocks and reduce the yields on bonds and cash over a longer term. Lower rates will start a new credit cycle, and perhaps a new real estate boom.

But all of this is many years away. For now, we must keep our eyes on potential global inflationary pressures and the so-called moral hazard being created by the Federal Reserve in its attempt to alleviate the subprime liquidity crisis. In late 2007, for instance, Bear Stearns, Citibank, and Merrill Lynch wrote off tens of billions of dollars in bad debt because they let greed get in the way of sound business sense.

Being aware of the facts is the best, first step to financial well-being. Certainly, by the time the direction of events becomes generally apparent, it will be too late for most people to capitalize on these developments. The proverbial horse will already have left the barn. To take advantage of these trends, investors should work with advisors who respond to the situation by restructuring their portfolios in a timely, considered, and appropriate manner.

2.5

Is It Time to Refinance Your Mortgage?

Ronald W. Rogé

As interest rates continued to fall over the last number of years, reaching an all-time low in 2003, we received calls from clients about refinancing their existing mortgages. If refinancing is a question that's been on your mind, it's important to speak with your current mortgage lender to see if that approach makes economic sense for you. It's also important to shop around and interview several mortgage lenders because there are many important variables in your decision-making process, including different back fees.

Before you shop for refinancing, you need answers to the following questions:

- What rate of interest are you paying for your current mortgage?
- What was the original term of your mortgage?
- How many years are left on your mortgage?
- How long do you plan to live in your home? (The answer to this question will help determine the type of mortgage—fixed, variable—that may be appropriate for you.)

Here are some other suggestions to keep in mind:

- Always shop for rates without paying points. That way you can get accurate interest rate quotes and can compare them.
- Ask for an estimate of total closing costs. Those costs can vary significantly from lender to lender and will be a major variable in determining the payback period (i.e., the period of time it will take to break even). The shorter the payback period, the better. So don't forget to ask your lender for a payback calculation.

Now that you have all the information, what should you do with it?

One strategy is to take an existing 30-year mortgage and refinance it to a 15-year mortgage at a lower interest rate. This approach assumes you will be in the home for at least five more years and the interest rate spread is

> *Reducing your mortgage term from 30 to 15 years is a form of forced saving.*

economical, with a long period of time remaining on the existing mortgage. Refinancing down to a 15-year mortgage is particularly effective for younger couples with young children facing college costs in their future. The strategy is to keep the monthly payments level, or lower, if possible, and pay off the mortgage in 15 years—at just about the time your children are ready for college.

Reducing your mortgage term from 30 to 15 years is a form of forced saving. It builds equity in your home and that equity provides flexibility you can use to supplement the savings shortfall for such things as your children's college tuition. This strategy makes sense for anyone wanting a mortgage-free retirement. If you plan to retire in the next decade or two, we encourage you to get your home paid off as quickly as possible.

With interest rates so low, some people are now looking for ways to make money using the equity in their homes. We've recently fielded inquiries from clients who want to take out a home equity loan and invest the proceeds in the market. In our business, this is called leverage. We don't advise you to take this path. If the market were to decline—which, as I showed in the previous chapter, is all too likely—you would lose the proceeds and be stuck paying off the loan. In some cases, people using this strategy have lost their homes or have been forced back into the workplace after retiring—a very sad outcome.

2.6

The 22-Year Car Loan
(Or How to Finance a Newborn's College Education)

Ronald W. Rogé, with contributions by Christine Parisi
and Jeff Roberto

One day I was eating lunch with my colleagues when one of them, Jeff Roberto, who is the father of three children, thanked me for giving him an article on how much it costs to raise a child these days—about $1 million, according to the calculations used.

Our conversation quickly turned to the cost of a college education, which can constitute a significant portion of the expense of rearing a child. I turned to another coworker, Christine Parisi, and observed that she could probably think of a college-savings program as a 22-year car loan. That's because saving for a newborn's college education from birth is equivalent to making 22 years of car payments.

With this thought in mind, Christine crunched some numbers for her daughter, who was born in December 2006. She used the cost of attending a private college today—approximately $40,000 a year—as her baseline assumption. Christine also factored in a 6% rate of inflation (the historical average for college tuition inflation) and an 8% return on investments. She then repeated the calculation using $20,000 a year—the average annual cost to attend a public college.

Here are the results:

College	Number of Years	Annual Tuition	Total Cost	Lump Sum Payment	Monthly Payments
Private	4	$ 40,000	$471,194	$113,248	$872
Public	4	$ 20,000	$235,597	$56,624	$436

This table shows that funding four years of college is a huge expense for most households. To meet the cost of a typical private college, one can make an initial investment of $113,248 or a monthly payment of $872 for 22 years. For a public college, the numbers are less daunting but still a challenge, requiring a lump sum investment of $56,624 at birth or monthly payments of $436 per month for 22 years.

With these figures in hand, Christine decided to have some fun (if it can be called that) with Jeff. She ran the numbers for his three children—aged 12, 9, and 7—for both private and public schools. In order to pay for a college education for all three of his children, Jeff's monthly savings number for the next 14 years would have to be $1,894 for a public college or $3,789 for a private one. The poor fellow was understandably in a state of shock. "What's a family with three children to do?" he asked. "Hope for scholarships, I guess."

Christine pointed out that, as far as car payments go, those college numbers are in Porsche and Maserati territory. For many American families that have more than one child, they are likely out of reach.

Even scarier, many of our clients are now faced with additional graduate school expenses. Today's children have it so good that there is almost no incentive to leave academia. After all, they don't live at home and someone else continues to pay their bills.

My goal in sharing this story is to underscore the fact that coping with responsibilities and expenditures of this magnitude requires long-term planning. The sooner you start a focused savings program, the better off you'll be down the line—not only financially, but also in terms of peace of mind.

In addition to encouraging them to save, I counsel younger clients who are buying homes to take 15-year mortgages rather than conventional 30-year loans. The idea here is for a person to have the mortgage paid off by the time his or her first child enters college. It also means that home equity can be tapped, if needed, to supplement the savings accumulated for a child's college education.

If you implement a timely and realistically structured tuition savings program, you might be pleasantly surprised when the time comes to send your future Nobel Prize winners to college.

If you implement a timely and realistically structured tuition savings program, you might be pleasantly surprised when the time comes to send your future Nobel Prize winners to college. You'll have accumulated assets and built equity in your home, and maybe your little wizard will conjure up a scholarship or two.

3 | Investment Strategies

3.1

The 10 Commandments of Investing
Ronald W. Rogé

1. Thou shalt recognize cash as the cornerstone of all investment programs. Use cash to establish an emergency fund equal to three to six months of living expenses before investing in any other type of security. Part of the planning process requires having funds set aside so that, in an emergency, you would not be forced to sell securities intended for long-term investment.

2. Thou shalt establish a time horizon for each financial goal, and establish separate portfolios for short (under three years), intermediate (three to 10 years), and long-term (greater than 10 years) goals. Invest with a goal in mind; never lose sight of your purpose.

3. Thou shalt establish an appropriate asset allocation for each of these portfolios. You should divide your portfolio into asset classes; for example, equities, fixed income, and cash equivalents. Never put all your investable assets in one asset class. Acknowledge the human emotions of fear and greed. Avoid chasing the performance of current hot sectors.

4. Thou shalt diversify your holdings by industries, sectors, companies, investment styles, capitalization sizes, and geographies, both domestically and internationally. If investors had done this with their portfolios from 1999 to 2001 and not invested entirely in technology and telecom stocks, they would have felt much better about the extended bear market.

5. Thou shalt consider the amount of risk associated with the return of each investment and compare it with similar investments in its category. All investments have risk. You need to assess the risk-adjusted return a potential investment has before investing in it.

6. Thou shalt monitor your asset allocation and periodically rebalance the portfolio. Once you have established an asset allocation that is appropriate for your goals and risk tolerance, the portfolio's asset allocation must be monitored and rebalanced when necessary. This will help maintain and control the amount of the portfolio's risk exposure.

7. Thou shalt not invest in companies without earnings. When you buy shares of a company without earnings, you are speculating, not investing. Most people cannot afford to speculate.

8. Thou shalt not invest in any security (stock or bond) without performing thorough research on that company, unless you delegate this task to a qualified professional. If you are unwilling to spend the time necessary to educate yourself and perform the work necessary to do the security analysis, delegate this task to a qualified professional.

9. Thou shalt be a good shepherd of your portfolio by paying attention to its longer-term performance and costs. Also, be sure to harvest losses in order to offset gains. This will minimize your tax bill and help build a higher net worth with better after-tax returns.

10. Thou shalt not seek stock recommendations from neighbors, friends, or brothers-in-law. In addition, thou shalt not compare returns with these people. They will only tell you about their winners. Your brother-in-law's stock tips will cost money. Period! Avoid this at all costs. People like to brag about winners. They are usually people who don't have a clue as to how their entire investment portfolios have performed. The only thing they can talk about is the quick profit they made on one trade. They won't confess to the 16 losing trades they made before the gain on that single trade.

3.2

Emotion Is the Enemy of Reason
Ronald W. Rogé

I was having lunch with my dad at his favorite restaurant, Zan's Kosher Deli in Lake Grove, New York, when we got to talking about the different ways people handle stressful situations.

My dad—now in his late 80s—is a highly decorated Marine who served in World War Two. Among other distinctions, he received the Bronze Star with a "V" for valor for his bravery in the battles at Saipan, Tinian, and Iwo Jima. You might say my dad is a real expert on stress—more than 6,000 Marines died on Iwo Jima alone.

Dad retired a number of years ago from a career as a textile designer. I always thought of him as an artist and nature lover; I never thought of him as a philosopher. But as he ages, he continues to surprise me in many ways.

As we ate our lunch and continued to discuss why some people can be so emotional under stress while others are quite unemotional, Dad suddenly said, "Son, emotion is the enemy of reason."

And it's true. Fear and greed are two strong emotions that tend to cause short-term market volatility. Benjamin Graham, the father of value investing, was fond of saying that "in the short term, the market is a voting machine; in the long term, it's a weighing machine." In other words, people vote with their emotions in the short term, but over the long term, a more analytical process takes shape. This analytical process permits a more productive interpretation of data or evidence.

On January 14, 2000, the Dow Jones Industrial Average Index (DJIA) hit an all-time high of 11,722.98 as a result of what then-Federal Reserve Chairman Alan Greenspan had a few years earlier called "irrational exuberance."

Fear and greed are two strong emotions that tend to cause short-term market volatility.

That's a polite way of saying "greed." Technology and telecom companies, some without actual earnings, were trading at sky-high multiples. The majority of those price run-ups occurred between 1998 and 1999.

In March 2000, rational thought began to weigh measures and compare values, and the long correction in prices began. It took almost six years for the Dow to recover from the decline and reach a new high. Does that mean people did not make money in the markets from 2000 to 2006? The answer is "no."

Those who stayed calm and collected during the rough patches were successful. Those who panicked and sold out missed a wonderful opportunity to significantly enhance their portfolios over the longer term. Even if they'd taken their diminished, post-correction assets and parked them in money market funds or treasuries, they still would have lost purchasing power from 2000 to 2006. Money market funds yielded from 1% to 2% during much of that period. While inflation was also low, those who panicked lost purchasing power on an after-tax basis. But more important, they lost the opportunity to recoup their losses because the market has moved dramatically higher since the beginning of 2003.

My dad's philosophical musing reminded me of something he had told me earlier, during that three-year bear market from 2003 to 2006. Dad is not a financially savvy person and had never spoken to me about the stock market, but during those rough markets he said, "Son, you would make a great Marine officer. You're so calm and cool in stressful situations that I'd follow you into combat without question." You have to realize this must have been a really tough thing for a Marine to say to a navy guy! So I know he really meant it. And it got me thinking about how to remain unemotional when the markets become difficult and challenging.

First, start with information—but filter it for the real knowledge. There is too much information being provided around the clock by our nation's many and diverse media outlets. Most of this information can be safely ignored. Scan the financial, business, and political news for details you might actually use about specific companies or market sectors.

Get to know people who are thoughtful, rational, and likely to have real knowledge about situations that have the potential for financial impacts. Listen carefully to these influential people, who might be money managers, journalists, business owners, or academics.

Also try to gain a global perspective. I start my day by scanning the *Wall Street Journal* and London's *Financial Times* to get a good perspective on world events. My son, Steven, and I read research papers written by people we respect and who have proven

A solid planning and investment process is the single best way to remain unemotional during stressful market fluctuations.

themselves over time. We attend meetings with these people and ask lots of questions; that way, we're able to assimilate all we have learned and draw our own conclusions.

A solid planning and investment process is the single best way to remain unemotional during stressful market fluctuations. When markets decline, especially over several months or even years, it's only natural to try to limit losses. It's very hard to sit tight. Yet, most of the time, sitting tight is the best thing to do because taking action is usually tantamount to trying to time the market. Bitter experience has shown market timing to be a losing strategy, even for professional investors.

The steadying influence of a process can be comforting when the market is declining. That's because an intelligent process provides discipline, stability, and continuity.

Thanks, Dad! The pastrami sandwich, knish, and Dr. Brown's Cream Soda were good, but the conversation was even better.

3.3

What Is a Market Index?
Ronald W. Rogé

The human brain has trouble dealing with complex problems or situations, so it looks for ways to simplify matters. Creating an index that is representative of the data it contains is a way to simplify.

> *To the financial world, an index is nothing more than a tool or a shortcut for handling a large amount of information.*

The most relevant definition for an index from the *Encarta World English Dictionary* is "a scale, or a number on a scale, that expresses the price, value, or level of something in comparison to something else or to a previously established base number."

To the financial world, an index is nothing more than a tool or a shortcut for handling a large amount of information. On the news every night, you hear the Dow Jones Industrial Average Index (DJIA) was up or down for the day. Dow Jones & Company, Inc. calculates and publishes the index in the daily newspaper, the *Wall Street Journal*, and in the weekly publication, *Barron's*. Investors watch the DJIA to monitor the stock market's performance.

But do you know what the DJIA is and why it's so popular? Do you know why most news media consider it to be the index to use when reporting to the public?

In 1884, Dow Jones & Company first published an index of 12 stocks, nine of which were issued by railroads, which were then the cornerstone of the United States economy. In 1896, the company published the first DJIA. The DJIA is today the most widely reported US stock market performance indicator. It is an average value of the stocks of the 30 largest blue-chip firms trading on the New York Stock Exchange (NYSE). These 30 companies are among the largest in the world. They include such giants as General Electric, General Motors, AT&T, IBM, Intel, Microsoft, Walt Disney, and Bank of America.

The DJIA, therefore, is a measure of the performance of the stocks of very large corporations that operate in every important sector, except for transportation and utilities. Editors of the *Wall Street Journal* pick the stocks listed in the DJIA. Those stocks are most often changed when a business undergoes major restructuring or is acquired by or merges with another business. However, with well over 7,000 domestic stocks actively traded in the US, the DJIA is no longer a fair or representative index of the overall market.

Why, then, does the DJIA remain so popular, and why is it still reported as the index that represents how the market performed on any given day? The answer to both questions is likely the same: because the DJIA was the first published index on the stock market. It's a matter of habit and tradition.

The second most popular index, sometimes reported in conjunction with the DJIA, is the Standard & Poor's 500 Stock Index (S&P 500). The McGraw-Hill Companies publishes this index, which is supposed to measure the ups and downs of the primarily domestic market by adding the stock prices of 500 designated corporations, and dividing that figure by a number that takes into account how many shares of each company's stock are available. The resulting average is reported in points, not dollars. Most of the 500 corporations used for the calculation are large, widely recognized firms. They include about 400 industrial companies, 40 financial companies, 40 utility companies, and 20 transportation companies. As you can see, the S&P

500 offers a more representative sampling of the stock market than does the DJIA.

Investment managers and other financial professionals most often use the S&P 500 to measure the performance of the stock market on a daily, weekly, and yearly basis. This index has become a benchmark against which the performance of many investments can be compared. Thus, a mutual fund might advertise that it outperformed the S&P 500 in a given year.

But the S&P 500 also has problems. Because it is capitalization-weighted (i.e., the values of larger companies carry more weight), any changes in the values of larger companies dominate the index and misrepresent what's happening to the whole market. This type of misrepresentation happened in 1998, when the S&P 500 increased in value by 26.67%. According to Laszlo Birinyi, (a respected market researcher and the founder and president of Birinyi Associates in Westport, Connecticut) in 1998, just 14 stocks accounted for half of that 26.67% gain. Many of the remaining stocks in the S&P 500 actually lost value. As a result, the S&P 500 did not accurately represent the domestic stock market in 1998.

There are other indices you ought to know about. The Wilshire 5000 Index measures the performance of more than 7,000 US companies. Given that it is capitalization-weighted, even this index has a large-stock bias. However, there is less of a large-stock bias in the Wilshire 5000 than in the S&P 500 because it represents more stocks.

In a perfect world, we would have an index that gives equal weight to each stock it includes. This type of index is sometimes referred to as an "arithmetic index" (Value Line publishes one). An arithmetic index, however, inevitably overstates the performance of its stocks, as a result of the daily rebalancing of the stocks in the index to maintain equal weighting. No one in the real world rebalances his or her portfolio on a daily basis. However, because of a statistical oddity, an index that gives equal weight to each stock's percentage change is upwardly biased for performance.

Some mathematicians recommend correcting this bias by using logarithms to determine the proper weighting for each stock's percentage change. The result is called a "geometric index," which results in a downward bias for performance (i.e., the opposite effect of an arithmetic index). Value Line also publishes a geometric index called the Value Line Geometric Index.

So, what's an ideal index? The answer lies somewhere between the arithmetic and geometric indices. In 1999, Mark Hulbert, a stock market performance tracker and statistician, suggested using an average of the two to measure the performance of a stock portfolio. I agree. Or, if you're looking for an index that will give you the most meaningful indicator as to how the stock portion of your portfolio is performing compared with the overall market, I recommend using the Wilshire 5000.

3.4

Mutual Fund Fees Matter ...
But Not as Much as You Think

Steven M. Rogé

How important are expenses in considering whether or not to buy a mutual fund? That's one of the questions inquiring investors are apt to ask. The short answer is that expenses matter because they have an impact on return. The slightly longer, but more relevant, answer is that, while fees are a factor, they should be weighed in the context of a fund's performance record and its manager's demonstrated abilities.

Like any business, mutual funds incur costs that encompass the administrative, investment management, legal, accounting, and marketing aspects of the operation. Fortunately for investors, those costs are conveniently bundled together as a single number—the expense ratio.

Here is a look at some of the fees that might arise when you invest in mutual funds:

- **The 12(b)-1 fee:** Together with the management fee, the 12(b)-1 fee is the principal component of the expense ratio. Originally intended to help with marketing efforts to grow assets, and thus benefit shareholders through economies of scale, this fee is increasingly being used to pay distributor servicing expenses—essentially a sales charge. Obviously, while one shouldn't divert 12(b)-1 income for unauthorized purposes—and we suggest you avoid large funds that still charge a 12(b)-1 fee—these funds should still be looked at with an eye on the larger context of performance and management ability.

- **Load funds:** Loads are not fees but sales charges. Fortunately, there is a way to avoid these extra costs and still benefit from superior load funds. You can do this by working with a company that gives you access without the expense—also called no-load access.

- **Performance-based fee:** A common feature in the hedge-fund world, this type of fee is now gaining some traction with mutual funds. Rather than paying a manager a fixed amount regardless of how his or her fund performs, a performance-based fee rewards a manager for generating returns in excess of a stock market index or other benchmark. It's an acknowledgment that, when a fund disappoints, its manager owes it to investors to share some of the pain. The concept of linking performance to fees (as long as they're not excessive) is a useful incentive.

Funds also generate brokerage charges, which are reported separately. This fee increases in overactive funds that turn over frequently. To avoid this often unnecessary expense, it's best to favor funds that employ a value-oriented, buy-and-hold approach, which implies a low turnover of holdings.

The quality and experience of a fund's management will have a higher impact than fees on the fund's record and return over time. So perhaps a better way to understand the impact of fees is to look at how a fund justifies its expenses.

The expense ratio for a typical actively managed stock fund is about 1.5%. We take note of a fund's expense ratio; even more, however, we look at a fund's total return over time. For instance, if a fund has outperformed its index by 500 basis points, or 5%, over the past five years, an expense ratio of, say, 1.75% doesn't have much of an impact. That's especially true if a fund's asset base is still small, because expenses are likely to decrease over time. If the expense ratio is above 1.75%, we look more closely at what might justify that level of cost.

A better way to understand the impact of fees is to look at how a fund justifies its expenses.

An area that relates to expense is performance history. To understand this element, most advisors screen for three- or five-year track records. It might, though, be worthwhile to seek out newer funds with seasoned managers who have solid records, either with other funds or in supervising separately managed accounts. Newer funds have other advantages: they're typically small and relatively unknown, thereby providing a greater degree of flexibility to uncover profitable inefficiencies in the marketplace.

Newer funds generally don't invest by committee, because they are more likely to leverage the insights of talented managers efficiently, providing an edge over other, more cumbersome, funds. Also, they define their own philosophy, control their investment process, and often pursue opportunities off the beaten path.

While such funds commonly carry higher expense ratios—at least until they accumulate larger asset bases—they also tend to generate better returns. That's because it's easier to beat market averages with a small pool of money than a big one.

The bottom line: while fees are important, they should not be the only factor you use when selecting a fund. Sometimes a higher expense ratio is actually a modest price to pay in return for access to a bright manager with the latitude to explore more freely the market's complexities in search of value and market-beating performance.

3.5

Individual Bonds or Bond Funds: Where Should You Put Your Money?

Ronald W. Rogé

I've always preferred the use of individual bonds, instead of bond funds, for the majority of the fixed-income portions of my clients' portfolios. In this chapter, I'll tell you why.

Individual bonds have a maturity date, which is the date on which a bond holder receives back the par value of his or her bond. Individual bonds also have a fixed-income stream; most bonds pay interest twice a year. The interest payment (the coupon) is set when a bond is issued. This means that owners receive a fixed coupon payment twice a year, despite any changes in interest rates. When a bond matures, its owner also receives the par value, usually $1,000 per bond.

Bond funds essentially create a poorly performing equity. The fund format eliminates a maturity date and removes the fixed coupon payment. Bonds in a fund produce only variable income. In other words, bond funds introduce two new elements of risk: lack of maturity date and variable payments. Plus, there's the expense of running a fund, which must be added to what is already a known commodity: the interest rate. That's right, interest rates are a commodity because they are public knowledge. To overcome the two risk elements and the higher expense, a bond fund manager must take additional risks just to break even with the current rate of interest. That's because bonds are designed to be low-return, low-risk investment vehicles.

Of course, there are some exceptions to the rule of buying only individual bonds. We use individual bonds for what we call our "plain vanilla" bonds: treasury, government agency, and municipal bonds. None of these bonds carries the risk of an individual business or enterprise.

We use bond funds under special circumstances, such as when we're buying:

- High-yield bonds (so-called "junk bonds")
- Convertible bonds
- Corporate bonds
- Bonds that produce phantom income

Bond funds are also worthwhile when the value of an account is too small to include several bonds with laddered maturities (e.g., a small individual retirement account [IRA]).

Generally speaking, high-yield, convertible, and corporate bonds should produce higher returns over time; however, there is risk associated with the individual business or enterprise issuing them. These bonds have a 4% to 6% average annual default rate. Imagine

> *Bonds are designed to be low-return, low-risk investment vehicles.*

investing a large sum of money in a high-yield bond and having it default. All the money invested would be lost, and the loss could have a material effect on the return of your entire portfolio. For this reason, if it's appropriate for you to own some of these riskier categories, it's best to diversify by holding them in a mutual fund. An individual bond defaulting in a fund that holds 100 different bonds will have less impact on your portfolio's overall performance.

3.6

To Hedge or Not to Hedge

Ronald W. Rogé

Hedge funds are private pools of capital that are basically limited partnerships. The money manager is usually the general partner, and investors are the limited partners.

The current vogue for hedge funds has caused this once arcane corner of the investment world to grow exponentially. Assets under management doubled between 2001 and 2006, reaching $1.4 trillion spread among 9,200 funds. Hedge funds once required you to be rich and put up big bucks to invest. Because of these constraints, participation in hedge funds has been limited largely to institutions and "accredited investors"—otherwise known as "the wealthy."

After the three-year bear market of 2000 to 2002, during which some people lost up to 80% of the value of their stocks, investors were looking for ways to avoid repeating their mistakes. The investment banking industry listened to what investors were asking for, and figured out a way to market a long-short strategy in hedge funds and make it available to the average investor. The pitch was simple: make money in up markets by being long in equities in part of your portfolio, while also making money in down markets by being short in equities in another part of your portfolio. Then, add leverage (borrowed money) to magnify the return on your portfolio.

You might expect the word "hedge" to imply caution, but the reality is that the typical hedge fund employs strategies with a wide variety of risks.

Next, the industry figured out a way to drop the minimum investment from $1 million to $50,000, so more people could participate. Suddenly, mere mortals with modest sums could act like big-league investors. A problem, though, is that big-league investors can afford to lose $1 million without losing any sleep. Joe Investor, who puts up $50,000 in one fund, can't afford to do the same.

Because they're unregulated, hedge funds can pursue all kinds of strategies that, for good reason, are off limits to conventional mutual funds. You might expect the word "hedge" to imply caution, but the reality is that the typical hedge fund employs strategies with a wide variety of risks.

Here are some of the more common risks associated with hedge funds:

- **Lack of transparency:** You don't know what you've invested in. In April 2007, the *Financial Times* reported, "Three-quarters of loans to junk-rated U.S. companies are now provided by hedge funds and other non-banks." Hedge funds use leverage to lend money to junk-rated companies. It's an accident waiting to happen.

- **Lack of information on how historical returns are calculated:** What method was used to calculate returns? Are the returns net of all fees? For unpriced securities in the portfolio, who made the valuations and what method was used to define the values used in calculating the historical returns?

- **Lack of disclosure:** Investors don't know who has side deals in the fund. They might be second-class investors but not be aware of it.

- **Lack of liquidity:** With ordinary mutual funds, investors can access the net asset value of their shares on a daily basis. But hedge fund investors may face significantly longer periods during which they are denied access to their money—in some cases up to two or more years.

- **Steep fees:** These fees are generally 2% annually on assets under management, and 20% on profits. Hedge funds, however, do not share in the losses. That's why it's often said that the best way to benefit from a hedge fund is to run one.

- **Lackluster performance:** Analysis has demonstrated that, because of high fees and other cost factors, it's unlikely investors will improve their long-term performance by putting money into hedge funds. Also, hedge funds are a prime example of a lot of money chasing very few ideas.

- **Assuming unacceptable risk:** High risk is a component of high return to justify outrageous fees. Hedge funds need to produce returns of 18% to 20% to give the limited partner a 10% return.

- **Lack of diversification:** Because they are making large, focused bets in the hope of outperforming and justifying their fees, hedge fund managers cannot realistically diversify.

- **Potential loss of capital:** Hedge funds blow up. Remember Long-Term Capital with two Nobel Prize winners on its board? Remember, more recently, the $9 billion Amaranth Advisors problem?

- **Leverage:** This is sometimes as high as eight times a hedge fund's capital. One wrong investment decision can make your money evaporate faster than the average investor can say "derivative."

- **Complex securities:** Hedge funds are fond of investing in complex or opaque investments (e.g., derivatives, options, futures) and deploying investment strategies that are not fully disclosed (e.g., short selling, betting on currencies).

- **Complex tax issues:** Accountants love hedge fund investors during tax season. Their summer vacations are financed by them. In general, hedge funds tend to be inefficient because of high levels of trading that rack up lots of taxable capital gains, not to mention the K-1 form needed before tax returns can be filed, but won't be received until late in the season.

- **Hedge funds are focused on numbers, not people:** An investor's goals and time horizon are irrelevant to hedge fund managers. Those managers are also indifferent to a person's tolerance for risk.

- **Scant knowledge of the hedge fund manager:** A manager may have recently closed a failed fund or may have run afoul of regulatory authorities. In a setback for investors, in 2006, a Federal Appeals Court struck down a Securities and Exchange Commission (SEC) rule that would have forced most hedge funds to disclose the names and any criminal records of those running the funds. In fact, hedge fund managers are not obliged to be registered investment advisors.

- **Requires expert due diligence:** Don't try hedge funds at home, folks. An investor needs expert help in performing due diligence on a hedge fund. And, even then, because of the problems I've already stated, an expert can still get it wrong after performing thorough due diligence.

The fad for hedge funds has increased SEC concern about unqualified individuals who lack the sophistication to identify and analyze the high-stakes strategies that characterize hedge fund investing. Accordingly, the commission proposed new rules in December 2006 that would require investable assets of $2.5 million—assets in stocks, bonds, or real estate, as long as the real estate is an investment property and not a person's primary residence—for hedge fund investors.

The current rule requires a net worth of $1 million, including the value of your primary residence, or two consecutive years of income of $200,000 (or $300,000 for a couple's combined income). In 1982, when the $1 million accredited investment threshold was defined, 1.87% of

> *The investment community understands the pull of emotions and creates products that play on them.*

American households qualified. By 2006, largely because of the appreciation of real estate assets, 8.47% of American households qualified to invest in hedge funds. Under the SEC's proposed standard, eligibility will shrink back to 1.3% of households. As of September 23, 2008, this proposed rule change is still under consideration by the SEC.

Now that you know about the common risks associated with hedge funds, what can average—but practical—investors do to achieve the performance necessary to meet their long-term financial objectives?

If you want to feel confident your portfolio will meet your expectations of generating reasonable returns that meet your time line and tolerance for risk, and let you sleep well at night, then follow these three steps:

1. Construct a portfolio that's right for you. Start by allocating assets in a balanced way among stocks, bonds, and cash. The point of diversification is to avoid having all your eggs in one basket.
2. Use mutual funds. Employ a mix of diversified and focused funds in your portfolio—and avoid hedge funds. The benefits include:
   - Full disclosure
   - Full transparency
   - A public track record
   - Regulation by the SEC
   - Lower fees
   - Diversification

- A smaller potential for loss because of diversification, lower fees, and asset allocation strategies
- Little or no leverage, thus lowering your portfolio's risk
- Avoidance of major tax issues
- Generally improved potential to realize your goals

3. Seek professional advice. Enlist the help of an experienced advisor to construct and manage your portfolio. A mutual fund manager will not know you, but your advisor will. He or she will know your needs, tolerance for risk, and your time line. A professional advisor who acts as your fiduciary will not select investments that are unsuitable for your situation. Today, there are mutual funds that use strategies that may be similar or identical to those of hedge funds—but without all the negatives.

While it's useful to highlight the issues associated with hedge funds, it also serves to underscore the challenges for ordinary investors who, from time to time, may be tempted to allow emotion to cloud their judgment. The investment community understands the pull of emotions and creates products that play on them; it's doubtful, however, that these products will provide any meaningful contribution to your investment objectives. They are usually pricey and risky, and stand very little chance of delivering on the promises made in the sales pitches. As always, do your homework and exercise a healthy degree of skepticism. As the well-worn saying goes, "If it sounds too good to be true, it probably is."

3.7

The Pros and Cons of Annuities

Rosanne W. Rogé

In this age of insecurity about markets and the world's outlook in general, individuals are always looking for a "safe" place to invest hard-earned dollars. Many financial service providers are playing on this insecurity, found particularly in the elderly. They tout annuities—either fixed or variable—as the best solution to allay investors' fears.

Tax-deferred annuities are expensive insurance products, and we do not recommend using insurance products as a substitute for investments. We recommend purchasing annuities directly and thereby avoiding paying insurance expenses.

There are various types of annuities. **Single premium deferred annuities** are funded with one lump sum or through flexible premium payments, and the money is withdrawn at a later date (preferably after age 59½, when there are no penalties). **Variable annuities** are composed of mutual funds in a tax-deferred wrapper. **Immediate annuities** require an insured person to deposit a specified sum of money with an insurance company. The

An annuity provides a stream of income that the annuitant cannot outlive.

insurance company then pays a monthly income for life or for a certain number of years.

Annuities carry several advantages:

- **Superannuation:** An annuity provides a stream of income that the annuitant cannot outlive.

- **Earnings:** Earnings compound on a tax-deferred basis.

- **No contribution limits:** Unlike individual retirement accounts (IRAs) and 401(k) plans, there is no limit on the amount of money that can be invested in an annuity.

- **Supplemental retirement income:** Systematic withdrawals from an annuity can provide supplemental income for retirees. This income is in addition to Social Security and pension income.

- **Death benefit:** If an annuitant dies before the annuity payments begin, the beneficiary will be paid a death benefit equal to the amount of the premiums paid or the accumulation value of the contract. The gain, however, is taxable as ordinary income to the beneficiary.

- **Nursing home protection:** Medicaid applicants who purchased annuities on or after February 8, 2006, are required to name the state as a remainder beneficiary to recoup medical costs once the recipient has died. The state must be named as a remainder beneficiary after the community spouse and/or minor or disabled child; otherwise, the annuity shall be treated as a transfer of assets for less than fair market value and may delay Medicaid eligibility.

Under the new law, for an annuity purchase to be considered an appropriate transfer of resources, it must meet the following requirements:

- It must be irrevocable.
- It must be non-assignable.
- It must be actuarially sound.
- It must have payments made in equal monthly amounts.
- It must exclude any deferrals or balloon payments.
- It must be purchased with retirement or IRA funds.

Please seek the advice of an estate planning attorney to ensure the purchase of this type of vehicle coincides with your Medicaid or estate planning.

If you are shopping for annuities, you should be aware of a few key points:

- **Fees:** Annuities can be very expensive because there are several layers of fees, such as administrative, insurance, and mortality fees. Insurance, administration, and mortality costs average around 1.27%; sales commissions run between 4% and 6%; annual contract maintenance fees are from $30 to $50 per contract; investment management fees run from 0.3% to 2.5%. There can also be a surrender charge up to 7%; this fee reimburses the insurance company for the commission paid to the broker who sold the annuity. If you purchase a variable annuity, you will also face mutual fund fees, and you may be charged to transfer between investment options.

- **Taxation:** While all annuities are tax-deferred, the earnings are taxed as ordinary income upon withdrawal. Upon your death, the annuity will be included in your estate for estate tax purposes, and it can be taxed at a rate of 45% (as of 2008). In addition, your beneficiaries will receive substantially less because of the income and estate taxes that are due. Unlike an insurance policy that pays out tax-free to your beneficiaries, the entire amount of an annuity is taxed as ordinary income, not capital gain income. As a result, your beneficiaries will probably lose one-third to one-half to taxes.

Annuities can be very expensive because there are several layers of fees.

- **Withdrawal:** Annuities are not very liquid before age 59½. That's because there's a 10% Internal Revenue Service (IRS) penalty for early withdrawal, in addition to ordinary income taxes.

- **Reinvestment risk:** In a fixed annuity, the interest rate is guaranteed for a minimum number of years. If interest rates increase, you are locked in at the rate at which you purchased the annuity. To reinvest the funds at a higher rate, you would need to surrender the annuity and pay the penalty.

- **Assumption of risk:** The holder of a variable annuity assumes the reinvestment risk associated with the investment decisions. Investment results are variable and not guaranteed.

- **Financial health of issuing insurance company:** Look for a financially stable and highly rated insurance company before considering an annuity purchase, especially if the annuity has a long-term horizon.

We recommend purchasing a non-qualified annuity only after you have maximized all funding for qualified retirement vehicles (e.g., employee tax-deferred accounts, such as 401(k), 403(b), and 457(s)). If, after funding all of your retirement sources, you're still in the market to purchase an annuity, we recommend using companies such as Vanguard, Charles Schwab, or TIAA-CREF, which have annuity products with lower fees and few or no surrender charges.

3.8

How to Decimate a Retirement Portfolio in Three Years

Ronald W. Rogé

People who are financially secure often advise those who are not to invest everything in stocks because stocks are tax-efficient and, in the long run, give a better return than bonds or money market funds. While this advice is sound in theory, it's impractical for the average person. These wealthy people are projecting their own needs and attitudes about money onto less financially secure individuals.

First, let's define financially secure. In my professional opinion, someone who is financially secure has a portfolio of $10 million or more. To help illustrate my point, I know an estate planning attorney who works with financially secure clients. He once asked me if I knew the difference between a person with $10 million and a person with $200 million. I was tempted to answer "$190 million." Instead, I said, "No, what's the difference?" He replied, "An art collection."

This attorney's point was that once you get past a certain threshold and you've purchased all your essential and dream items, the rest is play money to support hobbies or just to own things because you can. A person with a portfolio north of $10 million and whose goals are modest can probably benefit from a portfolio of mostly stocks, because he or she can withstand the hand of fate that may be dealt during the first three years of stock investing.

What do I mean by "the hand of fate"? I'm referring to the probability of one's portfolio producing a specific return during the first three years of investing. Take a deck of cards and on each card write the stock market return for each of the last 52 years. Shuffle the deck and deal yourself three cards. This will be the hand that fate will deal your portfolio returns for the next three years.

Let's look at Client A, a person who walks into our office with a $2 million portfolio. Assume Client A is retiring today and expects to live for 35 more years. He wants to produce $160,000 per year in retirement income while giving himself a 4% raise (to account for inflation) each year. Client A thinks his request is reasonable because, after all, that's only an 8% return and stocks have seen an 11% annual return over a 50-year period. This client has heard he'd get the best return and minimize his taxes by buying growth stocks. So we follow his advice and set up his portfolio.

For simplicity's sake, let's assume going forward that Client A is so tax-efficient that he owes no taxes (although that's highly unlikely because there are bound to be some dividends and capital gains in even the most tax-efficient portfolio). At the beginning of the year, Client A withdraws $160,000 to live on during the first year of retirement, and we invest the remaining $1,840,000 in growth stocks. The stock market produces a loss of 30% by the end of the first year.

Client A's portfolio is now worth $1,288,000 at the beginning of year two. At this time he withdraws $166,400 for expenses, which leaves the portfolio's starting sum at $1,121,600. The stock market rebounds and provides a positive 25% return at the end of the second year.

The portfolio has grown to $1,402,000 at the beginning of the third year. Client A withdraws $173,056 to live on, leaving $1,228,944 in his portfolio. The stock market returns 3% by year's end.

The portfolio has grown to $1,265,812 at the end of year three. In the beginning of the fourth year, Client A withdraws $179,978, leaving a portfolio balance of $1,085,834.

As a result of Client A's withdrawals and the stock market's performance, the portfolio has been reduced by almost half in just three years. The remaining $1,085,834 will not support Client A's original goal of spending $160,000 per year, increasing at 4% annually, for the next 35 years.

Now, let's compare Client A to Client B, who arrives with a portfolio valued at $10 million. Client B also wishes to withdraw $160,000 in the first year and increase this amount by 4% each year thereafter.

As tables 1 and 2 show, after the first three years, the financially secure Client B's portfolio is 17%—or $1.7 million—below its starting point of $10 million.[1] However, Client B still has more than enough capital to continue supporting his retirement goal.

TABLE 1 CLIENT A——NOT FINANCIALLY SECURE

	Beginning Balance	Income Withdrawl	Portfolio Balance	Rate of Return	Ending Balance
Year 1	$2,000,000	$160,000	$1,840,000	-30%	$1,288,000
Year 2	$1,288,000	$166,400	$1,121,600	25%	$1,402,000
Year 3	$1,402,000	$173,056	$1,228,944	3%	$1,265,812
Year 4	$1,265,812	$179,978	$1,085,834	0%	$1,085,834

TABLE 2 CLIENT B——FINANCIALLY SECURE

	Beginning Balance	Income Withdrawl	Portfolio Balance	Rate of Return	Ending Balance
Year 1	$10,000,000	$160,000	$9,840,000	-30%	$6,888,000
Year 2	$ 6,888,000	$166,400	$6,721,600	25%	$8,402,000
Year 3	$ 8,402,000	$173,056	$8,228,944	3%	$8,475,812
Year 4	$ 8,475,812	$179,978	$8,295,834	0%	$8,295,834

1. Both clients withdraw their money at the beginning of the year and their income needs increase at 4% each year in order to keep up with inflation.

Because no one knows or can accurately predict what a portfolio will return over any three-year period, we need to employ other strategies for the under-$10-million crowd. It shouldn't come as a surprise that this approach focuses on the following factors:

- Defining your goals
- Determining your portfolio's time horizon
- Defining your risk tolerance
- Knowing what your tax situation will be during your retirement years.

Once you know these factors your financial advisor can develop a plan that will give you a strong probability of achieving your goals.

Part of the plan will involve giving stocks enough time to develop their compounding magic. This means that stocks need at least a five-to-10-year time horizon to do their part in a retirement portfolio. Asset allocation will also help control your portfolio's volatility, and intelligent portfolio tax management will minimize your tax bill. The examples we used had only one year of negative stock market returns. Just imagine what two consecutive negative years of such returns would do to a newly retired investor!

We also assumed there would be no tax consequences arising from these sample portfolios. As you can imagine, taxes would only make things worse for both clients. While it's difficult to argue against an investment strategy that minimizes or delays taxes, taxes ultimately come due in one form (capital gains and income taxes) or another (estate taxes).

> *Stocks need at least a five-to-10-year time horizon to do their part in a retirement portfolio.*

The moral of our story is that investing an entire portfolio in stocks and selling stocks to produce income is acceptable only if your goals are reasonable and you have enough capital to declare yourself financially secure.

3.9

Do Better Than Break Even with Diversification

Ronald W. Rogé

I once spotted an article in *Barron's* magazine about the Standard & Poor's 500 Index (S&P 500). The article retraced the index's losses from March 2000, when it hit a record high, to May 2007, the so-called breakeven date, when it closed at a new record high. This period included the three-year bear market that began in March 2000.

The *Merriam-Webster* dictionary defines "breakeven" as "the point at which cost and income are equal and there is neither profit nor loss."

A person who invested $100,000 in the S&P 500 in March 2000 would now, more than seven years later, have $126,000 in his or her account. That's better than breakeven because I factored in reinvested dividends, which the *Barron's* article did not do. For comparison purposes, using the time value of money, consider that an investment earning a modest 5% total return annually over seven years would have made the account worth about $141,000 today.

So, should investors be satisfied with this standard benchmark's performance? They might, if they thought they had recovered their original investment. But while there is virtue in preserving capital, most of us don't invest with the goal of staying even. For that reason I think it would be useful to demonstrate that, in terms of purchasing power, the return of the S&P 500 was in fact much less than satisfactory.

Even though the original investment of $100,000—without dividends—had a 0% return over this period, the accrued dividends had a compound return of about 3.3% when reinvested. This result highlights the important difference dividends can make over time when reinvested back into a portfolio.

But a couple of other factors come into play that can affect a portfolio's value. For example, tame or not, inflation is always with us and it's constantly eroding money's purchasing power. Inflation averaged about 2.75% annually from 2000 to the end of 2007. As a result, what took $100,000 to buy back in 2000 required around $121,000 seven years later.

"Well," you might respond, "even with inflation, I'm still roughly at breakeven."

"But wait!" as they say in late-night infomercials, "there's more!" Another factor to consider is the value of the United States dollar, an aspect that has gained importance with the development of the global economy and the increasing globalization of securities markets. From 2000 to April 2008, the dollar's value slid about 95% against the euro and 22% against the DXY (the US Dollar Index), which charts the greenback relative to the value of a basket of major trade-weighted currencies. These changes translate into a decline of about 3% annually in global purchasing power. As applied to the original $100,000—factoring in total return, dividends, and inflation—the overall impact is a decline in international purchasing power to about $102,000.

In effect, inflation and weakness in the dollar more than offset the dividend gain. So, are we really at breakeven? Not remotely. We lost $19,000 (i.e., $121,000 in today's buying power minus the $102,000 value of the $126,000 portfolio, less currency loss).

Want to feel even worse? The bond market had great returns during this period. The $100,000 investment could have earned an annualized return of 6.25% in bonds, as measured by the Lehman Aggregate Bond Index. The $100,000 would now be worth more than $155,000.

Had the $100,000 investment been divided among stocks, bonds, and cash equivalents in a balanced portfolio using, respectively, the Vanguard 500 Index (60%), Vanguard Lehman Aggregate Bond Index (35%), and Vanguard money market fund (5%) during this period, the portfolio would have returned 4.31% annually and

> *Be smart and allocate your portfolio among stocks, bonds, and cash equivalents.*

would now be worth about $135,000. In addition, it would have achieved this result with much lower risk than an all-stock portfolio. This shows that asset allocation, diversification, and reinvesting dividends and interest pays off, even after a three-year bear market.

The lesson here is to not invest all of your money in one asset class or one basket of stocks—even if it's the S&P 500. Be smart and allocate your portfolio among stocks, bonds, and cash equivalents. Make sure your dividends are reinvested or reallocated in your portfolio, and be sure to have exposure to foreign stocks and bonds to protect your global purchasing power.

4 | Retirement

4.1

Baby Boomers and the Failure to Save
Ronald W. Rogé

According to several recent studies cited in *American Demographics* magazine, 67% of baby boomers worry about their financial future, and 68% say they haven't spent enough time planning for retirement. There's no doubt many boomers will find themselves with little or no savings when the time comes to stop working. Millions will be surprised to discover how meager their resources are.

Today's pre-retirees will have accumulated a median sum of approximately $380,000 by age 62. This total includes not only their savings but also the equity in their homes and the future value of their pensions and Social Security payments. Sadly, this amount is not enough for the majority of older households to maintain current levels of consumption into retirement.

According to one reputable study I read, most grandparents of boomers did not retire—grandmothers were rarely employed outside the home and most grandfathers never stopped working. In 1950, 79% of men aged 60 to 64 were in the labor force, and 60% of men aged 65 to 69 were also working. At that time, male life expectancy at birth was a mere 65.

It's worth repeating that, while the parents of today's pre-retirees led us to believe they saved money for retirement, in reality they never saved much. They actually lucked out and experienced a rare burst of generosity from the government and business. Medicare was put into effect in 1966 and Social Security was indexed to inflation in the early 1970s. Employers improved health care benefits and instituted generous pension plans. In addition, hyper-inflation caused housing values to shoot up as baby boomers entered the market. As a result, it felt like workers were saving a lot of money in the 1970s and 1980s. According to *American Demographics*, however, most of their wealth accumulation was in government and business promises. Therefore, the previous two generations did not instill healthy savings habits in today's pre-retirees.

It's been estimated that today's pre-retirees who are not participating in old-fashioned defined-benefit pension plans need to accumulate a minimum of $1.5 million in today's dollars (not including home equity) to supplement their Social Security payments. If this number seems shocking, remember that all 401(k) and regular individual retirement account (IRA) savings are taxable upon distribution. It's safe to assume that income taxes will consume 30% to 40% of those assets upon distribution. In addition, retirees need to increase their expense estimates each year to offset inflation.

So, while the invested portion of a portfolio is growing during retirement, expenses and income tax payments are being withdrawn at an ever-increasing rate over a longer-than-expected life expectancy. Over the next five to 10

The previous two generations did not instill healthy savings habits in today's pre-retirees.

years, the stock market will likely return to a more normal performance range; therefore, today's pre-retirees should not expect the stock market to bail them out of their responsibility to save for retirement.

Instead, pre-retirees will most likely need to save a painful amount of money each month to meet their retirement goals. Getting started today is the smartest move because the problem will only increase exponentially over time and painful savings now will become excruciatingly painful later on.

4.2

Overfund Your Retirement Goal to Comply with Noah's Rule

Ronald W. Rogé

Predicting rain does not count—building an ark does.
—Warren Buffett

Back in the 1980s, there were all sorts of articles written about how much money baby boomers would inherit from their parents and what great retirements they would have because of those windfalls. What those articles missed were previously unheard-of social and cultural changes:

- There are retired people today whose parents are alive and require the retirees' financial support.

- Many boomers must deal with so-called boomerang children, the sons or daughters who got married, had several children, got divorced, and moved back in with their moms and dads just as retirement approached.

- Boomers are poor savers. Evidence of this is our national savings rate of 0%.

Why are boomers such poor savers? Blame their parents who were poor role models for fiscal discipline.

Baby boomers' parents had defined-benefit plans (i.e., old-fashioned pension plans), which, by and large, do not exist in today's globally competitive labor market. They also had Social Security, which was a significant percentage of their pension income. Social Security for boomers will not be nearly as significant in providing the retirement income they will need.

Boomers' parents' homes appreciated significantly in value just as they were ready to retire and downsize. This allowed them to buy smaller homes and create investment portfolios using the balance of the funds remaining. While real estate has appreciated significantly over the past five years, it may not continue on this upward slope. In fact, it may depreciate over the next five to 10 years, just when the majority of boomers are retiring.

> *The moral of this story is to plan, plan early, and plan for the unexpected.*

The moral of this story is to plan, plan early, and plan for the unexpected. How do you plan for the unexpected? By implementing Noah's Rule[1] and thereby overfunding your retirement goal. It's no longer recommended that people be 100% funded at retirement to live to age 100. It's now essential to be 125% funded at retirement to live to age 100.

We are living longer in retirement, and so are our loved ones. To increase the probability that you will live your vision for retirement, this is the new model to follow. Any other plan could end in financial disaster.

---

1. See pages 35-36 for a full discussion of Noah's Rule.

4.3

The Top 10 Reasons People Don't Plan Properly for Retirement

Ronald W. Rogé

Creating a good retirement plan involves analyzing a complex situation that includes many variables. It's tempting to use mental shortcuts instead and simply imagine how your retirement might be. Whenever clients describe what they imagine and ask me,

The outcome of a retirement analysis almost always surprises people.

"Does that sound right to you?" my answer is always the same: "I don't know and won't know until I run your numbers." There are just too many variables to permit guesswork.

The outcome of a retirement analysis almost always surprises people. Sometimes those surprises are positive, but often people are very disappointed.

Here are the top 10 reasons people don't plan properly for retirement.

1. **Failure to consider the impact of inflation on the need for income.** At a 4% inflation rate, expenses will double every 17 years. A person might be retired for 30 years or more. During those three decades, his or her expenses will triple.

2. **Failure to consider the impact of taxes on expenditures.** With most retirees' assets in tax-deferred individual retirement accounts (IRAs), 401(k)s, 403(b)s, and pension plans, many retirees feel richer than they really are. They fail to consider that 30% to 40% of the distributions from these plans go to taxes in the year the funds are withdrawn. In our experience, retirees remain in their pre-retirement tax bracket until they begin receiving distributions from these tax-deferred plans to produce retirement income. When this happens, it's possible they will move into higher tax brackets.

We all expect to live forever, but when it comes to retirement planning we actually tend to underestimate our life expectancy.

3. **Failure to estimate non-recurring and irregular expenses during retirement.** The most often underestimated item is a car. Most retirees need to replace their cars every three to seven years. Another item is household maintenance, such as replacement of the roof, driveway, or boiler. Retirees need to include these items in their budgets and save for them.

4. **Failure to treat a mortgage properly in a retirement expense budget.** New retirees often have several years left to pay down their mortgages. Most assume their future expenses will be the same as their current expenses; however, once they have paid off their mortgages their expenses will be lower.

5. **Failure to properly estimate life expectancy.** We all expect to live forever, but when it comes to retirement planning we actually tend to underestimate our life expectancy. When we tell clients they have a shortage of capital and their portfolios will not last to age 100, they usually respond by saying they don't expect to live past 85. But a good retirement plan should extend to at least age 100. If a retiree lives longer than anticipated, who will support him or her during those last years? A 78-year-old client recently

called to discuss his mother's portfolio. His mother, who is 98 years old and sharp as a tack, wanted to know if she should have more growth exposure in her portfolio.

6. **Failure to plan ahead for disabilities.** Unfortunately, disability is frequently part of the aging process. Retirees should consider and plan how to pay for possible disability, either as a cash expense to be budgeted and paid out of pocket or as an insurance premium expense that's part of a long-term care insurance policy.

7. **Failure to plan for aging parents.** We see many retirees who, in the early years of their retirement, are caring for aging parents, both physically and financially.

8. **Failure to plan for boomerang kids.** Consider the couple who, after paying for their daughter's wedding several years ago, now plans to sit back and enjoy their grandchildren and retirement. Before that can happen, their daughter calls to tell them her husband has left her and, therefore, she and the kids will be moving back in with them. There goes that wonderful plan. Not only must our retirees support their daughter, but they also have two grandchildren to feed and babysit while their daughter goes back to work. It's tough to plan for boomerang scenarios, but it helps to have a cushion of excess assets just in case.

9. **Failure to understand the risks associated with investing in a retirement portfolio.** Understanding your needs, time line, tolerance for risk, income tax bracket, and diversification requirements for investing retirement assets is critical to achieving your retirement goals. Depending on your specific situation, it isn't necessarily wise to be conservative with a portfolio just because you are retired. That portfolio might have to work for the next 35 years and it will need to have a growth component to help achieve your income goals.

10. **Overestimation of a portfolio's long-term rate of return.** During parts of the 1980s and 1990s, stocks returned about 17% annually. Some of those years even saw averages above 20%. It's therefore not uncommon for prospective clients to consider a 15% or 20% return reasonable for a moderate-risk portfolio. When I suggest using a 6% - 7% return for planning purposes, clients look at me as if I've been in a coma for the past decade. I then explain that over the past 50 years the rate of return for stocks has been 11% annually, and that returns for bonds and money market funds are between 4% and 8% longer term. For planning purposes, returns on any portfolio with a blend of stocks, bonds, and money market funds must show a return below the 11% long-term rate of return associated with a 100%-stock portfolio. Experience has taught us that 6% - 7% is a reasonable and achievable return for a balanced moderate-risk portfolio.

4.4

The Death of Retirement as We Know It
Ronald W. Rogé

It's June 15, 2020. You've picked up your favorite newspaper to read on your way home. Its front-page headline says:

Today We Welcomed the Last Retiree on Earth

My guess is that this person would be a municipal or state employee. That's because the old-fashioned, defined-benefit pension plan has been almost eliminated from the private sector, and public sector employees will begin experiencing the very same fate over the next 10 years. The tax base can no longer support the generous pension plan benefits many teachers, firefighters, police officers, and other public sector workers have enjoyed in the past. We already see municipalities and teachers getting tiered plans—the higher the tier numbers, the less lucrative the pension plan will be.

Defined-benefit pension plans are the classic plans that companies paid for and employees assumed they were entitled to when they retired. The key word to remember here is benefit. Under this type of plan, upon retirement, employees receive a monthly benefit check for the rest of their lives. The check amount is based on a formula that factors in average compensation and years of service. This is the type of plan people usually associate with happy, secure retirees sitting in their rocking chairs on their front porches, contentedly watching the world go by.

Corporate America has effectively shifted the burden of contributing and managing retirement savings to employees.

My dear friends and neighbors, Ed and Shelly, are the perfect example of old-fashioned retirement. Both were elementary school teachers who taught in Brooklyn, New York, for over 30 years. Both retired a few years ago and are now enjoying the fruits of their labors on tier-one pensions. Ed and Shelly have a built-in cost-of-living provision in their plans. Which is a very powerful benefit to have as it means they needn't worry about the damage inflation can do to retirees on fixed-income pensions.

Both Ed and Shelly love being retired, and I love watching them. However, very few people in the private sector have the kind of defined-benefit pension plan my friends are enjoying. Over the past 25 years major corporations have gradually replaced these traditional plans with a 401(k) defined-contribution offering.

A **defined-contribution 401(k)** plan is the new savings vehicle of choice in corporate America. Companies are not required to contribute to these plans, although some offer to match a percentage of their employees' contributions. If a company matches contributions, employees are wise to take advantage of the offer. After all, it's free money.

The shift to a defined-contribution plan requires employees to make a conscious decision to save a portion of their salary, which is done on a before-tax basis (thereby avoiding income taxes) and grows tax-free until distributions begin. However, a 401(k) plan also requires employees to make investment decisions and manage their accounts.

Corporate America has effectively shifted the burden of contributing and managing retirement savings to employees. Employees are now responsible for their own futures. Not that they weren't responsible for their own futures before; however, in the past someone else could be blamed if the investments in a plan did not do well. If a company's pension plan failed, the government would take it over and make good on the funds. Employees had safety nets that no longer exist in 401(k) plans.

Companies say they are freezing and closing their defined-benefit plans because they're obliged to reduce costs in order to remain competitive. However, that wasn't the reason they gave two decades ago. At that time, they claimed they were replacing plans because employees didn't appreciate their valuable benefits. Employees, companies said, didn't understand how much money had to be contributed to these plans—in their minds, it was free.

The truth is that for an employee making $60,000 a year and having 35 years of service, his or her employer would be required to contribute somewhere in the range of $500,000 to $1 million in a defined-benefit fund—depending on variables such as age, pension formula, and current interest rates—to meet that individual's retirement liability. That's quite an expense for any company.

You alone are responsible for your future.

Because employees (especially younger ones) did not understand or highly value such pensions, many companies moved to eliminate them. (By the way, the same logic is now being applied to medical benefits. Most companies now require employees to pay a portion of their medical coverage, because when health care is free it's seemingly not appreciated.)

In recent years, several companies, including Verizon, IBM, and General Motors, announced they would be freezing their defined-benefit pension plans. As a result, employees will no longer receive credit for their years of service and the companies will cease to contribute to their plans. This development comes at the tail end of a process that has been taking place throughout corporate America for nearly three decades.

While this news is sending shock waves through the rank and file, these firms could have made their moves more than 10 years ago; however, they chose not to. Now, because of global competition, they have no choice. The end of defined benefits is especially painful to veteran employees who based their decisions to continue working at those companies on the superior compensation and benefits packages being offered.

The lesson in all of this? You alone are responsible for your future. The days of someone else funding your retirement are over.

4.5

Planning for the New Retirement
Ronald W. Rogé

A typical definition of retirement is "the state of having been taken out of use, considered of no further value."

In the cultural model I grew up with, retirees George and Martha sat on their covered porch in their rocking chairs and watched the world go by. This simple scenario is no longer valid. I don't know if it's due to a financial shortfall or just that the baby boomer generation wants to remain active longer and contribute to society in some meaningful way. Whatever the cause(s), this is what we hear from our clients today about retirement:

- I'd rather wear out than rust out.
- I want to phase out.
- I want to start a new career.
- I want to start a new business.
- I want to enjoy life fully, while continuing to contribute to society.
- I want to leave a legacy for my family or others.
- I want to run my own family foundation to help others in need.

We call it the New Retirement.

It's important to know what your goals are for your New Retirement. And it's equally important to figure out how to turn those goals into reality. The first step is to ask what we call the Big Visioning Questions. These questions are taken from the D.O.S. Conversation® and R-Factor Question® personal-thinking tools created and owned by the Strategic Coach®.

Over the next three years, what needs to have happened, both personally and professionally, for me to feel satisfied that I have made progress towards my goals?

Let's assume you'll live to be 100 and you have a 55-year future in front of you. To make the visioning and execution tasks manageable, we'll focus all of our attention on the next three years. Ask yourself, "Over the next three years, what needs to have happened, both personally and professionally, for me to feel satisfied that I have made progress toward my goals?" Your answer to this question will give you the guidelines for setting your objectives for the next three years.

Next comes the D.O.S. Conversation®:
1. What are the three biggest Dangers you face?
2. What are the three biggest Opportunities you have?
3. What are the three biggest Strengths you have?

Dangers might be:
- Poor finances
- Poor health
- Lack of human capital (i.e., ability to sell your services)
- Environmental concerns
- Family, friends, home situations

Opportunities might be:
- Start a new career
- Start a new business
- Improve your skills

Strengths might be:

- Significant assets
- Adequate risk coverage
- A plan for the future
- Good family relations
- A solid network of friends
- Willingness to embrace risk
- Excellent health

Now another set of questions needs to be answered:

- What's enough?
- How much money do I need at retirement?
- How long will the money last?

These are complex questions, with literally dozens of assumptions and variables to be taken into account. Some of the most common variables include:

- Age
- Life expectancy
- Income
- Expenses
- Taxes on distributions
- Inflation
- Types of assets

Once you've answered all these questions, you'll need to create a retirement budget.

HELPFUL TOOL

For help preparing your retirement budget, go to www.rwroge.com and click on the Financial Planning Tools tab. Then, download the Income and Expenditure Worksheet. You might also wish to download the Net Worth Worksheet.

If your company's pension plan allows for a lump sum pension distribution, you're lucky. Right now those distributions are in your favor because of the relatively low interest-rate environment that currently exists. That environment means a larger distribution for you. It's important to keep in mind that the distribution also becomes part of your estate. You own the assets, and they become part of your net worth. The lump sum distribution also eliminates the survivor option choice that some companies offer as part of their pension plans.

A lump sum distribution pension, however, requires you to manage your money prudently or get professional help to manage it. You need to be disciplined in knowing your budget and sticking to it, so that you won't run out of money.

When it comes to the survivor option these plans may offer, beware of pension maximization offers made by insurance agents in an attempt to eliminate the survivor option decision and save you money. The fact is you will probably not be sold enough insurance to do this properly. Also, it may be wise to consider a pop-up option if one is offered to you. A pop-up option allows your pension to increase if your spouse predeceases you. Choose wisely and get professional help. This is a very complex issue and your decisions are irrevocable.

Keep in mind that you are not alone in this endeavor. With planning and a little help from an advisor, you can create the New Retirement future you want. Yes, there will be obstacles. But, as Dan Sullivan likes to say, "The problem is usually not the problem. The problem is that we don't know how to think about the problem."

Many problems exist only in our minds. Our preconceived notions, attitudes, and beliefs get in the way. There is fear of the unknown and fear of changing. Mark Twain once said, "I've been through a lot of terrible things in my life. Some of them actually happened." He also said, "Twenty years from now you will be more disappointed by the things you did not do than by the ones you did do." Doing nothing is a choice, but not a very wise one.

4.6

A New Way to Fund Your IRA

Rosanne Rogé

For someone employed by a company, a tax refund is often the biggest lump sum of money he or she will receive in the course of a year. Thanks to the Pension Protection Act of 2006, taxpayers now have a way of splitting their

A split refund allows you to deposit your refund directly into one or more of three different types of accounts.

refunds into checking, savings, or retirement accounts. With the new split-refund option, you can pay some bills, save for an emergency, or save for retirement. Because it's important to save money for retirement, we advise many people to pay into an individual retirement account (IRA).

The split refund allows you to deposit your refund directly into one or more of the three different types of accounts mentioned above. If you wish, each of these accounts can be with a different financial institution. The split-refund option is available whether you file electronically or by mail, and you may continue to opt for direct deposit into one account by filling in the appropriate line on Form 1040.

There are two requirements for direct deposits:

- The financial institution(s) you use must accept direct deposits for your designated accounts.
- You must provide accurate account and routing numbers on IRA Form 8888.

Here are some important points to remember if you're going to deposit your tax refund in an IRA account:

- You are responsible for informing the IRA custodian of the year for which the deposit is intended. The Internal Revenue Service (IRS) will not indicate a contribution year for IRA accounts.
- If your financial institution denies a direct deposit, the IRS will issue that portion of the refund via a paper check.
- You should not exceed the annual contribution limits for IRA accounts. For the 2008 tax year, the traditional Roth and IRA contribution limit is $5,000. For those over age 50, the contribution limit is $6,000.
- It's up to you to keep track of your direct deposits, especially into an IRA. Contributions need to be made before the April 15 deadline.

HELPFUL TOOL

To track your refunds, use the IRS's free online service called Where's My Refund? You can access this service at:

http://www.irs.gov/individuals/article/0,,id=96596,00.html

Or call 1 (800) 829-1954

5 | **Financial Geriatrics and Estates**

5.1

Where Is Your Will?

Ronald W. Rogé

I was out of the office at a board meeting when I felt my cell phone vibrate in my pocket. After the meeting adjourned, I called my voice mail. My son Steve had left a message to call him—it was important. I could tell by the tone in his voice—most parents have this built-in radar—that something terrible had happened.

I called Steve and he said, "Dad, I've got bad news. Uncle Gary died earlier this morning." Gary was my former brother-in-law. I'd known him since he was 13 years old. No one expected him to pass away at age 56. While he'd had some medical problems over the past 10 years, Gary had continued to live a fairly normal life. When he passed away, Gary left behind two sons, my twin 28-year-old nephews, Ron and Mike.

Ron and Mike said their dad had told them he'd prepared a new will the year before, following a divorce. Ron, Mike, and other family members went through his home in search of that will but couldn't find it. They called lawyers whom Gary might have dealt with and still came up empty-handed. I knew Gary had prepared wills in the past, and I had no reason to doubt he had revised his will a year before he died, just as he had told his sons. But that knowledge didn't help us find the document.

The lesson here is that preparing a will is not enough. You need to tell your executor where the will is located, who prepared the will, and how to contact the person who prepared it. The original will should be kept with your estate planning attorney, not in a safe-deposit box. You should also file a copy of your will with your important papers.

Getting organized now means your family won't have an added burden during the stressful period that is bound to follow your passing.

HELPFUL TOOL

For a free organizer, go to www.rwroge.com and click on the Financial Planning Tools tab. Then download the Financial and Estate Planning Organizer. The organizer allows you to list, in one place, all your important documents, account numbers, and people to contact.

5.2

Young People Need Estate Plans, Too
Ronald W. Rogé

We all hope to live long and healthy lives. Sadly, though, that wish is not always fulfilled. It's therefore important to have an up-to-date will, living will, enforceable health proxy, and durable power of attorney.

Let's start with some definitions:

- A will is a legal document that declares an individual's wishes regarding the disposition of his or her property upon death.

- A living will is a legal document that indicates the level of care an individual desires should he or she become medically incapacitated. Living wills pertain only to life-support issues. Many states have passed living will legislation that allows a person to sign a document requesting that his or her life not be maintained through medical intervention.

- A health care proxy is a legal document that provides direction to medical providers regarding quality-of-life issues. With a health care proxy, an individual appoints someone (the "agent") to make medical decisions on his or her behalf if he or she is unable to do so.

- A durable power of attorney is a legal document that enables an individual (the "principal") to designate another person or persons (the "attorney in fact") to act on the principal's behalf at any time. A durable power of attorney is not terminated by the principal's disability or incapacity. Other powers of attorney are limited, allowing action on the principal's behalf only under very specific circumstances, such as while the person is out of the country. A springing (or non-durable) power of attorney becomes effective only under certain conditions, such as incapacity, which may have to be proven.

I wrote the first draft of this chapter in March 2005, when the media was filled with the story of Terri Schiavo. Terri was about 26 years old when her health problems first arose, putting her in a persistent vegetative state for 15 years. When the story broke, Terri was living out her last days after her parents had used and exhausted all the legal and political options to keep her alive. The whole crux of the case hung on hearsay—Terri's husband said she had verbally communicated her wishes to him. Terri has since passed away.

How many adults in their 20s have a living will and/or a health care proxy that will communicate in writing the specific measures that should or should not be taken to keep them alive?

The question I keep asking myself is how many adults in their 20s have a living will and/or a health-care proxy that will communicate in writing the specific measures that should or should not be taken to keep them alive? The answer is almost none. While the majority of our older clients have up-to-date wills, living wills, health care proxies, and durable powers of attorney, their adult children and grandchildren very often do not.

Furthermore, estate planning attorney Jed Albert, of Farrell Fritz (a Long Island law firm), points out that federal legislation enacted in 1996 requires the updating of all existing health care proxies and living wills. "The Health Insurance Portability and Accountability Act (HIPAA) deals with, among other things, the confidentiality of medical records." Albert says. He continues,

> Because of HIPAA, health-care providers may feel they can't share a patient's medical records with the individual appointed under a health-care proxy (the "agent"). If that occurs, it will be difficult for the agent to make intelligent medical decisions on the patient's behalf. Therefore, it is probably a good idea to revise existing health-care proxies. The new health-care proxies should contain language directing all health-care providers to give medical records to the appointed agents.

So, even if you already have a health care proxy, it should be updated to avoid any HIPAA medical record privacy problems.

While the Schiavo case gained national attention because it was being challenged legally in an effort to keep Terri alive, many people carry out wishes for their loved ones after death. In 2005, the *Wall Street Journal* ran a front-page article with the title "At 80, Mr. Hatashita Sails the Pacific Solo to Bring Wife Home." It was the seventh anniversary of Mrs. Hatashita's death, and she had always said she wanted to be buried in Japan, where she was born.

Mr. Hatashita sold his business, purchased a sailboat, took three days of sailing lessons and, at the age of 80, sailed 10,000 miles solo across the Pacific Ocean to carry his wife's ashes to Japan. Instead of taking a plane, he wanted to make a grand gesture to honor her, and he was able to use the time to be alone with his thoughts about her. When asked about the risk he had taken, he said, "Life is a gamble; you could have had a car crash—it's the same as that. If people think too much they won't move a single step." That's great advice from a dedicated and romantic widower.

While life is certainly a gamble, you can take the following four prudent steps to prevent a complicated and tragic event from placing undue pressure on your family:

1. Have all your estate planning documents reviewed to ensure they are current with the estate laws in your state.

2. Make sure your health care proxy and living will address the HIPAA issues I outlined above.

3. Ask all adult (18 and over) members of your family to have a will, living will, health care proxy, and durable power of attorney prepared. Younger people will probably not want to spend the money to get it done, so Mom, Dad, Grandma, Grandpa, or Uncle Harry may have to pay for the services—a very small price for peace of mind.

4. While many states have rules that honor out-of-state health care documents, if you spend considerable time in more than one state (e.g., New York in the summer and Florida in the winter), to play it safe you should have a health care proxy and a living will executed in each state's customary form.

It's difficult for most of us to think about our own demise and how we want to exit this world. However, if you don't communicate your wishes in writing beforehand, someone else will make choices for you and they may not be the choices you would want. Take the time now, while your mind is clear and you are not under stress, to do the difficult thinking, and document your choices with an estate planning attorney.

5.3

Right-Sizing Your Senior Lifestyle

Sally Allen and Rosanne Rogé

Difficult and often agonizing, it's the crossroad every senior dreads—the time when it's necessary to consider abandoning the comfort of the familiar for a more practical, age-appropriate living scenario.

This transition is often referred to as "downsizing," but we prefer to call it right-sizing. For most people, it's a difficult process, encompassing emotional and logistical issues, as well as a fundamental revision of financial arrangements.

Moving from one environment to another can result in relocation stress syndrome, defined as a state of physiological and/or psychological malaise. "Each time an older person finds it is no longer reasonable to live in his or her home or community, it is a crisis on an individual and family level," says John Rother, the director of policy and strategy for the American Association of Retired Persons (AARP). Seniors who prepare for the move using a

Moving doesn't get easier with age. Sooner is generally better than later and, as the saying goes, there's no time like the present.

specialized transfer team, and who maintain the same staff before and after the move, make a much better transition.

According to Sherri Melrose, PhD, in her article "Reducing Relocation Stress Syndrome in Long-Term Care Facilities," which appeared in the *Journal of Practical Nursing* in 2004, a successful transition hinges on a number of key factors:

- Developing a sense of personal control over the environment
- Having adequate time to prepare
- Minimizing differences between the old and new environments
- Being able to rely on a specific and highly trained team

First things first: When is it time to pack up the house? Obviously, the variables that go into making this decision differ for every family; bear in mind, however, that moving doesn't get easier with age. Sooner is generally better than later and, as the saying goes, there's no time like the present.

In undertaking this challenging task, careful planning and organization can make all the difference. Here are five helpful steps:

1. Take stock of your current situation. Figure out where you are, where you might be going, and what, if anything, is holding you back. Create a plan of action. Give yourself a realistic time frame and begin the process.

2. Arrange to have all the basic moving supplies you'll need. These include:
   - Boxes with useful labels such as Donate, Recycle, and Family (placed in strategic areas for easy access)
   - Trash cans and garbage bags
   - Markers, labels, rubber bands, and lots of tape

3. Besides making progress, the key consideration is to get things done in a way that makes you comfortable. Therefore, break the project down into manageable pieces and identify the priorities:

- Where do you want to start?
- What room or material should you tackle first—the basement, art and decorations, books, linens, clothes, small furnishings? Schedule one or two hours a day (or more, if you are so inclined) to work on a specific area.

4. Have your transfer team help you begin the difficult process of sorting and "editing" (we like the term "editing" better than "purging"), as well as collecting similar items together. Keep the treasures; let go of the "maybes." Sure, it's tough, but the bottom line is not to burden yourself and your family with things you want but don't need. Saying "Give it a hug and let it go" is a nice way of acknowledging that you want to keep the item but really don't need it anymore. It's easy to find a charitable organization that would be happy to accept your donations—that way, everybody wins.

5. Maintain your focus and discipline until the job is done—then celebrate!

Next, assemble the team that can see you through the rest of the process safely, efficiently, and—most importantly—with understanding and sensitivity. At this stage it's important to consider where and from whom you might find the right kind of support. These people will become your resource bank of contacts. They may include family members and friends, as well as relocation specialists, various tradespeople, real estate agents, and others.

The transition is a journey. Look for help along the way and make the most of your resources. If you feel it's too overwhelming, you can hire help. Throughout the country, there are experienced professional organizers who specialize in relocating seniors.

HELPFUL TOOL

The National Association of Professional Organizers can provide referrals to a professional organizer who can meet your needs. Visit its Web site at www.napo.net.

It almost goes without saying that another important component of the right-sizing process is getting your finances in order. Conversations about wealth take place on two connected levels: the practical and the emotional. The practical level revolves around basic considerations about how your money will be transferred. Equally important from an emotional standpoint are the "whys" of your decisions.

Your first financial decision will be to create a budget that reflects your new realities. In many cases, right-sizing frees up additional funds for everyday living because, in your new setting, you're unlikely to be burdened by any significant mortgage and home upkeep considerations. Utility costs, for instance, will probably be lower or even included in a monthly maintenance fee. These are just some of the reduced home expenses that may provide you with additional cash flow.

HELPFUL TOOL

For help developing an updated cash flow analysis, go to www.rwroge.com and click on the Financial Planning Tools tab. Then download the Income and Expenditure Worksheet.

As with any financial plan, the key is to pay yourself first. You should put a portion of the additional discretionary income generated by your new and more economical lifestyle toward savings. We recommend you keep at least three to six months' worth of expenses in a separate checking or savings account to avoid incurring debt in the event of an emergency.

Once you've settled in your new home, the time may be right to visit a financial professional to review your investments so that you are properly positioned for the future. It may also be time to visit (or revisit) an attorney to ensure you have all the proper documentation—including a will, living will, health care proxy, and durable power of attorney—to address any events that might arise. Reviewing and updating your legal documentation is especially important if you have moved to a different state.

Reviewing and updating your legal documentation is important, especially if you have moved to a different state.

Many seniors fear change, but change can bring great opportunities and a fresh outlook. It might seem overwhelming at first, but proactively adapting—or right-sizing—your lifestyle to better accommodate evolving circumstances will pay valuable dividends down the line, by more efficiently focusing your financial resources and promoting your peace of mind. So, consult with family members, friends, and trusted professionals, and then start planning for a new and better future—today.

HELPFUL TOOL

Visit www.SallyAllenOrganizer.com for tips and information on organizing and relocating seniors

5.4

"Permit" Me to Help You

Rosanne Rogé

Not all planning and preparing has a direct financial impact. Sometimes preparation will save you only time. But, as they say, time is money; so, here is a time-saving tip for those of us with caregiver responsibilities.

I frequently help my in-laws get to their doctor appointments, dinner functions, and other everyday destinations. Both Dad and Mom use canes and find it difficult to walk any great distance. I therefore always try to drop them off at the front entrance of wherever they happen to be going.

At one point I had obtained a special parking permit to help out my mother. It then occurred to me that it might be a good idea for my in-laws, too. I did a little research on our town's Web site and found I could apply for a handicapped parking permit, which would allow me to use one of those specially designated spaces that are located closer to the entrances of public buildings, such as stores, medical facilities, and post offices.

Getting such a permit is really quite an easy process. In New York State, for example, start by completing the first part of the application. The second part must then be completed and signed by the attending medical professional, who attests to the condition that necessitates the special parking permit (note: in most cases, only a medical doctor, nurse practitioner, or podiatrist may complete these applications).

Once you have filled out the application, simply submit it to the relevant municipal authority (e.g., the town clerk's office or the police department). In most cases, the permit will be issued a few days later. Be sure to verify whether you need to submit the application in person or by mail. And don't forget to take your license with you if you're the one doing the driving.

A few easy steps on your part can save many steps for your family member who may need a little assistance in getting where he or she needs to go. Your help will generate savings in time and effort that will be much appreciated.

5.5

The Case for a Health Care Advocate
Rosanne Rogé

In this busy world of ours, we all know how important it is to have timely information in order to make wise choices. We gather that information from sources such as the Internet, newspapers, magazines, and other periodicals. Often, we also reach for the telephone.

There are, however, some contemporary challenges that come with using this venerable device. Whether we're calling about insurance coverage, credit card information (e.g., stolen cards, limits, and payments), or just to make an appointment with a physician, we frequently get caught in automated attendant "hell." (I'm sure there are many other words that could be used for this place, but we need to keep this book printable!)

Frustration is an everyday reality when we're unable to speak with a human being about a problem and, instead, get tangled up in one of those labyrinthine automated attendant menus. Frustration and resentment are magnified when the labyrinth traps a senior who is trying to renew a prescription or get details about medical coverage for a particular test.

I recently had this experience with my father-in-law. The phone rang and it was Dad, in a state of alarm and confusion. He'd been trying to reach the outpatient department of a local hospital to schedule a CAT scan. The person scheduling the appointments checked Dad's records to verify his insurance, and then informed him he had no medical coverage.

Dad took out the insurance card from his wallet, called the member services number—and then it happened. The poor man was made to endure 20 minutes in automated attendant hell. He struggled, pressing every number he could in a vain effort to connect with a live person who might be able to provide assistance. Finally, in total exasperation, he just hung up and called me.

I assured him he was covered under Medicare, his primary carrier. Dad also has coverage under a supplemental health care policy that's part of my mother-in-law's retirement plan. I told him this policy would be in force because the premium payments are deducted directly from his wife's pension check.

With authorization, you will be able to act efficiently on the elderly person's behalf and make his or her life (and yours) a little easier.

In an effort to take the edge off the situation and get him to relax, I got directly involved. I spent about three hours on the phone trying to figure out what had happened; predictably, however, there were no easy answers. Going back and forth between Mom and the representative (the representative would not speak with me because I was not listed as a contact person), it finally emerged that Mom's coverage through her company had been changed to another carrier.

The representative on the phone was kind enough to connect me to an actual person at the new insurance company, and we obtained coverage information and new cards for Mom and Dad. While I had this "live one" on the phone, I asked her if there was any way Mom could appoint a "patient advocate" who could intervene should another situation like this arise. She told me that Mom and Dad would need to complete and sign a special form authorizing me or my husband to act on their behalf with the insurance company.

I recommend that anyone with elderly parents, parents-in-law, or grand-parents ask the insurance company, or any other relevant service provider, if they have a form to authorize the release of information and/or to designate a representative.[1] With authorization, you will be able to act efficiently on the elderly person's behalf and make his or her life (and yours) a little easier.

1. A form of this type is quite different from a health care proxy or durable power of attorney, which need to be completed with the assistance and guidance of an estate planning attorney.

5.6

How to Buy Long-Term Care Insurance

Rosanne Rogé

When it comes to long-term care insurance, there are three burning questions we are asked time and again:

1. What is it?
2. Do we need it?
   and the biggest question of all,
3. Can we afford it?

When we prepare a retirement analysis, we use a life expectancy of 100. Clients usually respond by saying, "You've got to be kidding!" But, thanks to medical advances and the increased attention given to such health matters as nutrition and exercise, the average life span is much longer than it used to be.

One hundred years is a wonderful milestone, but who will take care of you when you reach that ripe old age? Will the responsibility fall to your spouse, your children, the government, or you? Planning for that far-off future begins today.

For generations, it was a family member—customarily, the daughter or daughter-in-law—who took care of elderly or ailing relatives once they could no longer look after themselves, or when financial constraints did not permit them to live independently. Years ago, family members lived close to one another, and therefore nearly all could share in the caregiver role. Now, with both husbands and wives holding down full-time jobs and families spread throughout the country and sometimes overseas, the responsibility is becoming increasingly difficult to share.

> When we prepare a retirement analysis, we use a life expectancy of 100. Clients usually respond by saying, "You've got to be kidding!"

So what happens if there's no one nearby or available to look after you? The burden of your long-term care may fall on your own shoulders or those of your spouse.

Long-term care involves a broad range of supportive medical, personal, and social services to help people meet their basic needs for an extended period of time. These basic needs are known as the activities of daily living (ADL), and include eating, bathing, dressing, mobility, transferring (e.g., moving from bed to chair), toileting, and maintaining continence. When ADL care can't be provided by family and friends, a long-term care facility or life-care community is an option.

But no matter where or how care is provided, it can be expensive. For example, according to the New York State Partnership for Long-Term Care, in 2006 the average daily cost for nursing home care on Long Island was $347. Medicare's Part A pays for up to 100 days of skilled care in a skilled nursing facility. For the first 20 days, Medicare pays all covered services in full. For the next 80 days, you pay a daily co-insurance amount of up to $128 and Medicare pays the rest. After 100 days, payment is entirely your responsibility.

There are other parameters that can limit Medicare-covered benefits. All policies have "gatekeepers" who have the power to decide who is eligible for benefits. Gatekeepers are a critical part of every long-term care policy.

Under the best policies, a person qualifies for benefits when his or her physician orders specific care, such as skilled nursing or rehabilitation services on a daily basis. The individual must be in the hospital for at least three consecutive days

Because it's clear that Medicare can't be relied upon for true long-term scenarios, purchasing your own long-term care coverage is a wise choice.

and must be admitted to the nursing or rehabilitation facility within 30 days of being discharged from the hospital. Other policies require that care be "medically necessary for sickness or injury." In such cases, the insurance company determines who qualifies for care. Activities of daily living are a third type of criterion (more on them below).

Because it's clear that Medicare can't be relied upon for true long-term scenarios, purchasing your own long-term care coverage is a wise choice. When shopping for a policy, here are eight criteria you should consider:

1. **ADL:** These are the benefit triggers that will qualify you to begin receiving benefits under your policy. A person usually must be incapable of performing at least two of the seven ADL—eating, bathing, dressing, mobility, transferring, toileting, and maintaining continence—to qualify for benefits. Be sure that any policy you are considering covers cognitive impairment, such as Alzheimer's disease, senility, irreversible dementia, and mental dysfunction caused by stroke.

2. **Daily benefit:** This should cover both nursing home and home health care. It will give you the flexibility to remain at home and receive care, if desired. As mentioned earlier, the approximate average cost of a nursing home on Long Island in 2006 was $347 per day: that's the daily benefit amount. Be sure to do some cost comparisons of the nursing homes in your area.

HELPFUL TOOL

If you are fortunate enough to be covered under a long-term care plan through your workplace, take advantage of it.

---

3. **Benefit period:** This defines how long the benefits will last. A typical nursing home stay is between three and five years, so be sure your policy covers that period of time.

4. **Elimination period:** This is the waiting period before benefits start; it runs for 30, 60, or 90 days. During the elimination period, you are required to cover all costs out of your own pocket. The longer the elimination period, the lower the policy premium.

5. **Guaranteed renewable:** The best policy is one that is guaranteed renewable, which means that coverage will remain in force as long as the premium is paid.

6. **Inflation protection:** In order for a policy to keep up with rising nursing home or home health care costs, the best option is to have an automatic compound annual percentage increase in benefits. Policies also provide a periodic catch-up provision whereby a higher level of benefits can be purchased without evidence of insurability.

7. **Level of care:** Your policy should cover all levels of care, both skilled (nursing care) and non-skilled (e.g., for those ADL that do not require the assistance of a nurse, such as bathing and dressing). Ideally, benefits should allow for a nursing home, home health care, adult day care, or assisted living.

8. **Financial stability of the insurer:** You want a financially secure company to issue your policy. Research the financial ratings of prospective companies at your local library, through A.M. Best, Moody's, or Duff & Phelps. You can also contact your state insurance commissioner's office for a list of companies authorized to sell long-term care policies in your state.

Other provisions to look into will cost an additional premium but may be suited to your situation. These provisions include:

- **Spousal discounts:** If both spouses apply for coverage, there is usually some sort of discount on the premium.

- **Survivorship:** If both spouses apply for coverage at the same time and one spouse dies, the policy for the survivor becomes paid-up after a certain time period.

- **Restoration of benefits:** After the insured has been out of a nursing home for a certain period of time, full benefits are restored under the policy.

- **Bed reservation benefit:** A bed reservation benefit ensures the policyholder will not lose his or her nursing home bed during a hospital stay.

- **Respite care provision:** For those who receive health care at home, usually by a family member, the respite care provision provides the caregiver with some time off. Some policies provide for temporary nursing home stays, home health care by another individual, or adult day care for the insured.

Under the Health Insurance Portability and Accountability Act of 1996, your long-term care policy may be "qualified." This means policy premiums may be deducted as a medical expense on your income taxes, and the insurance benefits received are not taxable as income to the beneficiary. But there are a few criteria to meet:

- The policy must provide only for qualified long-term care services.
- The policy must be guaranteed renewable.
- The policy must not have a cash value.
- Any refund of premiums must be used to reduce future premiums or increase future benefits.

If you are fortunate enough to be covered under a long-term care plan through your workplace, take advantage of it. Because it's group coverage, you will pay less in premiums than if you purchased the policy on your own.

As with any insurance policy, the best time to buy is when you are young and healthy. Premiums increase as you age, and if you have an illness, you may pay high premiums for coverage, or not be insurable at all.

5.7

Assisted Living and Continuing Care Options

Rosanne Rogé

All across the United States the number of people age 65 and older is growing at a much faster rate than the rest of the population. Because of the strong desire among seniors to remain active, independent, and close to family and friends in the communities they have lived in all their lives, the construction of alternate living facilities has become a fast-growing industry.

There are a variety of living facilities available that can be matched to the physical care and support services seniors require. In this chapter, I focus on the two main types: Assisted Living Facilities (ALFs) and Continuing Care Retirement Communities (CCRCs).

I should note here that if you choose to live in an ALF or CCRC, long-term care insurance will not cover your expenses. For this reason, it is important to evaluate your goals and your personal situation well ahead of time to determine how you should structure your savings or insurance coverage.

Assisted Living Facilities (ALFs)

ALFs are neither nursing homes nor retirement communities; they are somewhere in between—on a middle ground between independent living and nursing home care. These facilities can be free-standing, part of a CCRC, or affiliated with a nursing home. They serve both individuals and couples, and come in all shapes and sizes.

Accommodations range from a separate apartment to a simple bedroom and sitting room with a shared or private bathroom. Basic services such as housekeeping, laundry, transportation, and recreational services are provided. Three meals a day may be taken in a resident's apartment or in the communal dining room. Help is provided to those individuals who need assistance with day-to-day tasks (e.g., dressing, bathing, and medication), but who are otherwise able to manage by themselves and don't need the full medical services of a nursing home.

Nursing personnel pay daily visits to check on residents regarding their medication and general well-being. One of the key benefits for most residents is a sense of security, knowing that medical personnel are available 24 hours a day in case of an emergency. Each ALF apartment is equipped with an emergency call button or other emergency alert systems to summon help.

ALFs are neither nursing homes nor retirement communities; they are somewhere in between—on a middle ground between independent living and nursing home care.

ALFs are popular with families and caregivers because they are less restrictive than nursing homes, which more often than not carry an uncomfortable stigma, and are the last places many older adults want to go. ALFs instead provide individuals with as much independence as they want or need and foster a greater degree of self-esteem and confidence, all at a lower cost than a conventional nursing home.

ALFs can still be costly, though, ranging from $1,800 to $6,000 per month. Rates and fee structures vary, depending on such things as the location of the residence, the size and style of the living unit, and amenities and services provided. When you're researching ALFs, ask for a written statement of the resident agreement, a document that will outline the services offered, prices, and extra charges. For example, is the rate structure a flat daily rate based on the amount of assistance needed or one price for all? Please remember that Medicare, Medicaid, and many long-term care insurers do not cover these facilities.

Federal laws and some state laws do not regulate ALFs. Of the 50 states, only 29 (plus the District of Columbia) regulate and license these facilities to ensure adequate care is provided to residents and ethical business practices are followed. Because there is little regulation, the quality of the facilities, staff, and services vary greatly. Be sure you visit the ALF, speak with the staff, and see how the residence is maintained before deciding if the facility meets your needs for care and independence.

HELPFUL TOOL

To find out more about ALFs, contact the Assisted Living Federation of America at (703) 691-8100 or www.alfa.org. You can also call Senior Alternatives for Living at (800) 350-0770. AARP has a wonderful booklet called Selecting Retirement Housing. It includes worksheets to help you determine if ALFs are right for you, both emotionally and financially. Visit www.aarp.org/family/housing.

Continuing Care Retirement Communities

CCRCs provide care for life and promise medical and nursing care when needed. As we age, our needs change. Couples and individuals must be ambulatory when they move to a CCRC; however, if they later become ill or disabled, certain nursing, health, and personal services are provided. Nursing homes and rehabilitation facilities are usually on the premises; if not, they are nearby. If the health needs of one spouse

CCRCs provide care for life and promise medical and nursing care when needed.

require that person be transferred to a health care unit, or if one spouse dies, the survivor may remain in the living quarters and be assured of uninterrupted care.

Living accommodations can be apartments, townhouses, or detached dwellings. Services also vary, and there is generally a choice of recreational, cultural, and social activities. A CCRC can be all-encompassing, offering libraries, beauty parlors, barbershops, banks, swimming pools, and tennis courts. Meals served in hotel-style dining rooms, housekeeping, transportation, and social activities are also included.

The CCRC concept all sounds wonderful; again, however, convenience has its costs and the costs are not covered by Medicare, Medicaid, or long-term care insurance. CCRC residents usually pay a one-time entrance fee (which may range from $200,000 to $600,000) in addition to monthly payments for services (which may range from $650 to $4,000) such as maintenance, housekeeping, meals, and health care. In exchange for these fees, residents are assured of housing and services for the rest of their lives, regardless of their health.

Typically, there are three types of CCRC contracts:

- **Extensive:** This contract type provides housing, residential services, and amenities, as well as unlimited long-term nursing care for little or no increase in monthly fees.

- **Modified:** This contract type includes all the housing and residential services covered by an extensive contract, plus a specified number of days of nursing care or long-term care.

- **Fee-for-service:** This contract type provides housing and residential services, along with some short-term nursing care.

A CCRC is a lifetime commitment. Before you sign, be sure to have your attorney, accountant, and investment advisor review the contract. Also, have a cash flow analysis prepared to determine whether your retirement income, sales proceeds from your home, and other funds will cover your CCRC expenses.

The medical affiliation of the CCRC you choose is very important. Therefore, check the hospital or health system that supports the facility.

Last, but not least, find out if the facility is accredited by the Continuing Care Accreditation Commission, the only accrediting body for CCRCs. Contact the commission via www.carf.org/aging, or call (202) 587-5001 or toll-free at (866) 888-1122.

HELPFUL TOOL

The Commission on Accreditation of Rehabilitation Facilities (CARF) offers free downloadable guidebooks for consumers. Visit www.carf.org and click on Free Publications.

Resisting the Lure

There is one remedy for the stress of living in complicated times: live simply. That is the fisherman's lesson. Now the task is figuring out how to apply that wisdom to our daily lives.

It is our hope that this book has expressed the values that shape the personal and intellectual qualities our team has been cultivating in our lives and in the lives of our clients. Overarching our personal and collective goals, there is a single theme all of us are working on. We are learning to resist the lure of today's complexity while embracing the peacefulness of simplicity in our lives.

Without even realizing it, most of us have allowed the great American marketing machine to tell us what we need, when we need it, and how much of it we need. Advertising is the bulk of our media consumption and media has saturated almost every public and private space.

In our never-ending pursuit of a more perfect life, we have allowed our finances to be overextended, given away our time, and eliminated our privacy. The noise and false choices of contemporary society distract us, ensnaring us in a life of urgency rather than importance.

And yet, should we look for them, there are hopeful signs of change everywhere. It is becoming clear that the marketing machine can pull us in only so far. After all, we are more than a herd of buffalo following its leader over the cliff in our pursuit of the bigger, better, faster, newer, media message.

We are a society seeking to recover the more meaningful and important things in our lives. We see evidence of this search for meaning in the trends that are emerging in our daily lives and in the global economy. People are taking back their time, privacy, and space.

Protecting Our Time

Thanks to mobile computing and telephony, everything from text messages to phone calls, from stock prices to headlines, can be delivered to anyone, anytime, anywhere. Our private and business lives are mixed together in the daily dance of schedules and interruptions. The time we spend at work catching up after participating in this instant communication madness has impinged on our time. This, coupled with longer commutes and traffic delays, means we spend less time with family and friends.

On the other hand, mobile computing and telephony technologies also make it possible to work from home. However, the distractions of the home environment may not allow us to focus on doing the job very well, leading to additional frustrations and bizarre work hours, where nothing in life seems normal anymore.

Another interesting development is an effort to reverse some of the socially damaging effects caused by technology. The rise of e-mail-free days in large corporations is an effort to get employees talking face-to-face again, instead of hiding behind e-mail communication. It is an effort to bring back some humanity to an office environment where workers rely too much on e-mail.

We have already used up a portion of our life's allotment of years. No one can say how many years remain, yet we all know the number is limited. It's up to us to carefully screen and evaluate every situation, request, and proposal that comes our way in terms of the time we have left on Earth.

Protecting Our Privacy

Privacy is perhaps our second most valuable possession—because when we allow advertisers to influence us, they are infringing on our first most valuable possession: our time. Here are some simple steps that can help protect privacy and time:

- Block e-mails you don't want, such as spam. We are big fans of a program called ChoiceMail. You can visit www.digiportal.com to read about it.
- Have a firewall on your computer to keep out unwanted intruders.
- Use software to clean your computer of adware and spyware files that allow websites you have visited to track your preferences.
- Block catalogs you don't want at www.catalogchoice.org. (By doing so, you also save trees and the fuel it takes to produce and transport all of those catalogs.)

Protecting Our Space

Have you noticed that space is becoming limited? Have you taken a plane ride lately? They are trying to get more people in less space to improve profitability. Professional organizers, space consultants, and clutter clearers are all services that didn't exist three decades ago. But with home offices moving into family homes, older workers downsizing, and retired people moving into seniors' apartments, there is a huge demand for help to sort through decades' worth of possessions, the emotions, and memories they evoke, and to clear the dust that has settled over boxes and boxes of unused stuff.

Those boxes of unused stuff filling basements, attics, and garages across the country illustrate the ultimate lesson of *The Banker and the Fisherman* perfectly. Live simply! It's just stuff, and we don't need it all, despite what the marketers may tell us. It just clutters up our space and the way we live.

Slow down. Focus on what's really important to you. Protect your time, privacy and space. In doing so, you'll be moving closer every day to a simplified life that feels more perfect for you.

As these new ways of thinking take root, we at R.W. Rogé & Company will be assessing how they will affect our lives and our future. We are constantly looking for ways to free ourselves from the complex messes we find ourselves in today. Doing so gives us the freedom to move toward a more simplified and meaningful life.

While we've reached the end of this book, this is not the end of our story. We are carefully watching these trends, welcoming them, and embracing them. You can follow our progress by checking our website www.thebankerandthefisherman.com, where we will be posting subsequent articles about living a more balanced and simplified life.

Authors and Contributors

Ronald W. Rogé, MS, CFP®

Ronald W. Rogé is a nationally recognized wealth manager. He is the founder, chairman, and chief executive officer (CEO) of R.W. Rogé & Company, Inc., a fee-only investment advisory firm organized in 1986. Ron has an extensive background as a corporate executive, having held positions in engineering, marketing, and corporate finance.

In 2005, *Bloomberg Wealth Manager* magazine selected Ron as one of Bloomberg's Top Wealth Managers. The *Robb Report Worth* magazine voted Ron as one of the Nation's 100 Most Exclusive Wealth Advisors in 2004. In 2006, *Investment Advisor* magazine chose Ron to head up the list of the 25 Most Influential People in the profession. Ron is frequently quoted by the media, including the *Wall Street Journal, USA Today, Business Week, Fortune, Newsday,* and *Money* magazine, and is often asked to lecture other advisors at conferences and trade shows.

Ron earned a bachelor of science degree from Long Island University and a master of science degree in business administration from Polytechnic University. He is a member of the National Association of Personal Financial Advisors (NAPFA) and the Financial Planning Association (FPA).

Rosanne Rogé, CFP®, CSA®, RFG℠

Rosanne Rogé is the managing director of Client Services at R.W. Rogé & Company, Inc. She is a certified financial planner (CFP), certified senior advisor (CSA), and registered financial gerontologist (RFG). She has held the National Association of Securities Dealers (NASD) series 6, 7, and 63 securities licenses and is a New York State life, accident, and health insurance licensee.

The media frequently seeks Rosanne's advice. She has been quoted in the *Wall Street Journal, Bloomberg Personal Finance* magazine, *Investment Advisor, Fortune, Newsday, USA Today,* and *US News and World Report.* She is a NAPFA financial services affiliate and a member of the FPA. Rosanne earned a bachelor of arts (*cum laude*) in human relations/psychology and an associate degree in applied science from Pace University.

Steven M. Rogé, CMFC®

Steven M. Rogé serves as portfolio manager at R.W. Rogé & Company, Inc., where he researches and analyzes investment securities.

Steven is a member of the New York Society of Security Analysts (NYSSA) and is the chairman of the NYSSA's Value Investing Committee. He is frequently quoted by national and local media, including *BusinessWeek*, *Newsday*, the *Wall Street Journal*, *Barron's*, and *Fox Business News*. Steven earned a bachelor of science degree in finance and economics from Bryant University and holds the NASD series 7 and 63 securities licenses.

Index